The Gulf Coast Collection
of Stories and Poems

GULF COAST
COLLECTION
of
Stories & Poems

Edited by
James P. White & Jeff Todd

TC
WP

TEXAS
CENTER
FOR
WRITER'S
PRESS

First Edition
Copyright 1994 Texas Center for Writers Press
Printed in the United States of America
TCWP
P.O. Box 428
Montrose, Alabama 36559

Hardback ISBN: 0-916092-20-8
Paperback ISBN: 0-916092-19-4

Copyright Notices and Acknowledgments

"Jamaica" by Angela Ball in *Partisan Review*, copyright 1990. Reprinted by permission of the author.

"Hawk of the Night" by Ewing Campbell in *Cimarron Review*, No. 101, copyright 1992. Reprinted by permission of the author.

"Staying Lost" by James Clark from *Dancing on Canaan's Ruins*, Ars Gratiis Publishers, copyright 1983. Reprinted by permission of the author.

In Memory of Sylvan Karchmer

Contents

Stories

Poems

Stories

Bastard

Allen Wier

At 2:22, the morning of September 12, the year 1944, I was born in the Medical and Surgical Memorial Hospital in San Antonio, Texas. My birth certificate lists the attending physician as C. H. Dittman, my weight as six pounds, eleven and one-half ounces. On back of the birth certificate are two tiny purple footprints beneath the declaration *Unchanging Evidence of Identity*--but I still have to accept these facts, like all history, on faith. This does not make me doubt what I believe I know about the past. That such knowledge is only educated speculation adds to the pleasure of drawing conclusions. I read what I like: geography, history, anthropology--land and lore. But I can bear witness only to what I remember.

It's a city now, but during the time I'm remembering, San Antonio was just a big town. They'd started building expressways, but for the most part my father drove us down narrow, crowded streets. Neon sombreros and cocktail glasses turned gravel parking lots lavender as the sun sank behind roofs and cast an orange glow over tourist courts shaped like the tepees used by Comanche Indians less than a century earlier. Used cars posed under strings of lightbulbs next to pink stucco gas stations and army-surplus stores. We rode past curb-service joints where girls snuggled close to soldiers in dark coupes parked beneath canopies, trays of burger baskets on the cars' windows; past honkey-tonks where doors were propped open and Mexican border music and willowy shadows sashayed out onto sidewalks to mingle with boys in tight black trousers who strutted like straight razors.

In those days, San Antonio did not host the conventions and tourists it does now. Near downtown, small frame houses, close to the streets and to one another, were separated in back by alleys lined with telephone poles and garbage cans. Here and there an oleander bush, dust whitening its poisonous leaves, grew against a screened porch. A few hackberries and one or two palm trees stuck up above the rooftops. These neighborhoods gave way to brick warehouses with steel casement windows along double and triple railroad tracks: my father's territory.

His line was Industrial and Commercial Janitorial Chemical and Maintenance Supplies: mops, brooms, brushes, detergents, cleansers, waxes, polishes, retardants and sealants. He told Fuller Brush Man

3

jokes. I figured he wasn't a great salesman, because my mother worked afternoons at a branch of the public library, and because he nearly always knocked off work around the time I got out of school. It was years before it occurred to me that he quit work early in order to be there when I got home.

Home, during the time I'm remembering, was a house we'd just moved into, in a new subdivision south of town where the hills flatten out and oaks give way to short mesquites and cactus. As soon as we moved in, we began clearing our lot of rocks. We laid out squares of carpet grass till our yard was a green and caliche-white checkerboard on which we guyed up a few live oaks.

Picture the straight streets and bare lawns, the identical rows of brick houses, to understand why my father got me up early one Wednesday morning--the beginning of April and already so hot I slept without covers, a window fan barely moving the stiff hairs of my flat-top haircut--to go with him to a building-supply house where he'd made a deal to swap three cardboard barrels of industrial cleanser for two sets of white aluminum shutters to decorate our front windows and mark the house. He was tired of driving down our street and not recognizing which driveway was his.

Worried that I would be late for school--I had a math test second period--I unlocked the door to the storeroom where my father kept the cleanser. I worked hard enough to sweat up my school shirt, wobbling barrels of the sweet-smelling red powder one at a time across the carport.

While my father finished a "quick" cup of coffee, I remembered the times I'd waited for him, all the times he'd taken me with him to make a "quick" call. I'd grown up listening to him tell his customers what a smart boy I was, *Not like his old man, no sir, takes after his mama, got her brains and her looks to boot.*

My mother was not pretty, but she had ways that made her seem so. She spoke quietly, as if working at the library made her forget how to raise her voice, and I often whispered words to her. Freckles splattered her face the way raindrops on a windowpane splatter a face with shadows. Her hair was the color of those freckles, her eyes between hazel and green, changing with her surroundings. I remember one hot afternoon planting and watering--a scarf tied around the back of her head kept her hair up off her sweaty skin, and her cheeks were smudged with dirt--my father knelt on the hard earth working a square of sod into place. He stopped and looked up at her, and I looked too. Her eyes were gold in the sun, and when she smiled at him, her eyebrows lifted and her face opened up. I like to think that for a moment I saw her as my father did.

My father was what my mother called *a nice size*--"not so big he looked dumb, but big enough to hold you tight." He had, she said, bedroom eyes and was a good dancer. "Oh, he was wild, your daddy was, and so good-looking. Plenty of girls envied me." More than once I heard her say she'd never know what made him fall for her, but I could tell by the way she smiled into her reflection in the window over the kitchen sink that she knew more than she would tell. And fall for her he had. At his funeral, as if I had asked her, she leaned over and whispered, "Your daddy was never unfaithful to me."

With me, he was a jokester, poking and punching like an awkward adolescent, mussing the top of my head like a distant uncle. He never knew when to quit. My cheek stung with the rub of his night-time beard, my shoulder slowly gave up the red fingerprints of his pinches and squeezes; recollections of him are burned, sore places--small aches that feel better in memory.

The morning I want to tell about, my father came out the kitchen door onto the carport, a white coffee cup he held to his lips covering his nose, mouth, and chin like a surgical mask. He slipped the empty cup to my mother in the space and the moment between the closing screened door and the jamb it slapped.

"What're we up to here?" he said--to me, to her, to himself, to no one in particular.

In her robe, behind the screen which dimmed her like an underexposed photo, my mother looked like she had not yet thrown off the fuzziness of sleep. With both hands she held his cup and watched my father back the station wagon down the drive and into the street where he hit the brakes--the taillights red as a secretary's nail polish-- and lurched forward, hit the brakes again and threw it into reverse, driving like a parking-lot attendant. The engine whined as he backed onto the carport, stopping when the bumper just touched my leg--*stop on a dime and give you change,* I'd often heard him say. I hefted the barrels into the back of the wagon.

As we eased down the driveway, our house got smaller in the mirror on my side of the car. Then we were going down the street and our house disappeared into all the anonymous others. My fingers were wrinkled from my long effort to wake up in the shower, and enough of the red cleaning powder had escaped the cardboard barrels to fill the creases in my skin. Both my hands looked lacerated.

A week earlier, I had gone with my father into one of the Gebhardt Spice Company's warehouses, chili-powder fumes burning my eyes and nose, and seen him demonstrate the cleanser--red dust, he called it. I'd watched him unbutton his sport coat and nod at Mexican workers who were pushing loaded dollies out to the truck docks. The Mexicans nodded back, smiled, spoke Spanish words to my father and to one another and kept working. My father's upraised left hand held a lid like a tambourine, his right hand disappeared into a cardboard barrel. He took a step back, dipped his head and swung his arm the way a magician bows and sweeps his arm out before a trick. Pixie dust, the red powder sprinkled through my father's fingers and spattered the concrete floor like droplets of blood. The Mexican men grew silent; they eyed a redheaded, red-faced man who had an oval patch sewn over his shirt pocket, the name *Andy* stitched there in script. Andy grinned and took his time shaking a cigarette from a pack of Luckies. The Mexican men stopped, eased their dollies upright and waited. The white pack of cigarettes with its round red label jerked and danced in Andy's hand in the dim light. Andy's match flared and he bent to his cupped hands, one eye squinted against the flame. He nodded once and breathed out smoke. The Mexican men stood silent, heads slightly bowed. Though I didn't see it then, I remember them as parishioners at mass. My father waited while Andy pinched the tip of his tongue, then held his hand down at his side and flicked his middle finger from his thumb like someone who had covertly picked his nose.

What came next embarrassed me then, though the memory of it does not. My father knelt to his sample case and took out the wide head of a sweeper broom and twirled it into a long handle he'd leaned against a stack of boxes. He hefted the broom and smiled in pantomime just as I'd once seen a clown hold a broom and smile. He gave it a shake, popped the sweeper head flat against the handle, then folded it out again, his eyebrows moving up as if to say, "Folds flat for easy storage." Then he bent and swept, silent and solemn as Emmett Kelly. Magically, he swept a swath of concrete clean as fresh-poured. Done, he brushed his hands together and rested them on his hips.

My father clapped Andy on the shoulder. I followed them to the office, where a woman named Shirley was making a fresh cup of coffee.

"Don't suppose that red stuff'd work in here?" Andy said, and he tapped his work shoe on the stained linoleum office floor.

"Do a bear shit in the woods?" my father said. Then he said, "Pardon my French, Shirley." He and Andy grinned, and Shirley leaned close to me, laughing a minty laugh. She offered me a Coke and a stick of Juicy Fruit. She put her hands, warm, on my shoulders, her nails red, red against my shirt, and then stepped back, her arms curved bridges from her shoulders across to me, held me as if waiting for music so we could begin to dance. Standing close, breathing her powder and perfume and feeling her heat, was like standing close to a cotton-candy machine, sweet-smelling and bright, lightbulbs warming the glass box that holds the pink cloud of spun sugar. If I were rude to Shirley, I knew, I would disappoint my father and turn his praises of me into lies. Shirley sat on the edge of her desk and crossed and swung her legs. Her stockings tightened and her legs whispered, and I watched light wiggle up her shins to disappear beneath her dress. Beside Shirley's typewriter lay two work gloves--both right hands--palms up, fingers curled stiff, two rough brown hands waiting to be held.

"I guess I'll go on outside and wait in the car," I said.

"Here," he tossed me the keys. When I reached and caught them, he caught my arm, gave me a hard squeeze. "Might be something you want to listen to on the radio." He winked at me as if he had invented radio, dreamed it up and designed it to work in our car especially for me. The radio was always on. The tuning knob turned all the way in either direction but the red line stayed on the same station--news and weather on the hour and half-hour, sales pitches and hit tunes in between.

The morning we headed down our street to get shutters, it was not yet eight o' clock. On the car radio a man's voice was forecasting the weather: more of the same--hot and dry. Then the morning business report came on, talk about stocks and bonds, utilities, the commodities market, and then something called *trading in futures*.

"Hey," my father said. He stopped hard enough that I grabbed the door handle. "Want to skip school today? Play hooky, hang out with your old man?" His hand was on my thigh, thumb and fingers squeezing above my knee until he found that soft spot that gives an electric shock, your leg's funny bone.

"I've got a math test."

He nodded, but I knew he was thinking, "Better yet, skip school and get out of a test."

There was a haze over the pavement, heat waves already wiggling up. We were on the Poteet Highway. As we got closer to town, traffic got heavier, loud through our windows rolled down for air. A pickup pulled in front of us, and my father hit the brakes, pitching me against the dash. He shook his head, didn't say a word. The pickup, an old Dodge, had been hot rodded and had had a recent, do-it-yourself paint job, glossy black. The rear was jacked up and two chrome exhausts puffed blue smoke. My father leaned toward the windshield, checking the highway ahead; he glanced at the rearview and pulled into the other lane. As we passed, I saw where someone had painted a big, gold bumblebee on the side of the truck bed with paint that looked like the glittery gold ink my mother had used with a quill pen for signing our Christmas cards. Beneath the chubby bee was the hand-painted word: STINGER. The truck's driver turned and glared at us. A kid--he was just a kid. He couldn't have been much older than I was. I wondered if he had a license to drive.

As soon as we pulled back into the right lane, I heard a loud drone. I looked behind us, but the Dodge wasn't there; it was passing us on the right, on the shoulder. Gravel pinged against our car and a sharp click left a tiny blue-green star on my side of the windshield.

"Goddamn," my father said, in the exact tone he'd say *Yes Ma'am* when my mother asked him to pick up a loaf of bread at the ice house, which is what convenience stores used to be called in San Antonio.

We went another mile, maybe less, and the road became four lanes. My father pulled alongside the truck. He turned to look at the driver but the kid stared straight ahead. His window was rolled all the way up, hot as it was, and I knew it didn't work. My father shook his head and smiled. "I hope you'll have better sense." He accelerated, and I was pressed back as the station wagon lunged ahead. The pesky black truck surged forward, too. "What're we up to here?" my father said. He slowed and the truck slowed. Then the truck began to speed up and slow down, speed up and slow down--a galloping horse, its black nose nodding as it rocked and bucked beside us. "Little bastard," my father whispered; he stared ahead with both hands on the wheel and looked as calm as a Sunday driver, except his knuckles were white.

The teen-ager driving the truck stared straight ahead, his face frozen, his lips pulled back exposing his teeth. It was a face I knew from a movie, an astronaut, lift off, G-force. We were so close I saw the pearl snaps on the kid's short-sleeved cowboy shirt, so close I was sure I could reach out and wrap my fingers around his door handle, open the door a crack, reach inside and touch the smooth skin beneath his ear.

I saw a yellow warning sign; then I saw the kid see it, too. He hunched forward. More signs: Construction Ahead, Right Lane Ends. The pickup nosed ahead; then we caught up. The truck angled toward us; we didn't veer or slow down. The kid turned his head my way, his eyes wide. My father did not move. The kid opened his mouth, closed it again.

I do not know if my father saw the warnings, though I don't see how he could have missed them. The black truck strained ahead again and started to nose past us. My jaw was clinched and my right foot pressed the floorboard. I wasn't going to let him cut in. "Bastard," I said. I think the corner of my father's mouth twitched with the faintest hint of a smile. "Bastard," I said, louder; the word felt good coming out of my mouth. Then we were speeding up, too. The kid looked right at me, looked at me as if he knew me.

I have no idea how long all this took. People often describe split seconds of crisis in terms of slow motion or stop action. This was not that slow. This seemed like regular life at regular speed with me seeing and thinking a notch or two faster. I believe nothing was lost on me that morning. On our left was a Mobil station, the winged horse flying slow revolutions above the roof; on our right a Brahma bull (everyone I knew said Bray-mer) the color of caliche stood alone behind three strands of barbed wire. The bull raised his head, high as the hump between his shoulders, his pendulous dewlap swaying. Behind him, the field turned white where it met the horizon.

Ahead, the pavement went over a dry wash, and there was a new concrete abutment--the reason the lane was closed. All the kid had to do was slow down. He had time to pull onto the shoulder, to pull over and wait for a safe opening.

The black truck swerved off the highway the way one of the fighter planes that buzzed our house from Lackland or Kelly Air Force Base would tip a wing and veer out of formation. The truck's front fender struck four fence posts, one after the other, *ack-ack-ack-ack*--a fighter plane, mowing them down, snapping them off close to the ground. Steel whips, long strands of barbed wire coiled and uncoiled, popped like anti-aircraft guns.

The pickup bounced sideways and almost stalled--rear wheels spinning dust and smoke--then roared, wheels digging in, and shot back onto pavement. It smashed through a wooden barricade, and my anger congealed into fear, cold and hard as a block of ice. The truck bore down in a way that looked intentional and butted into concrete. The engine stopped, and I realized how loud it had been. By then we had gone past, over the wash. My father pulled onto the shoulder and we got out. We stepped across new concrete. Neither of us ran.

Other cars had stopped. The truck's engine snapped and clicked, hot metal cooling. Steam came out from under the hood, and something red spilled onto the pavement--blood, I thought, until I smelled antifreeze. The window glass was cracked--a 10,000-piece puzzle. A man ran up from an old Studebaker Champion, his plaid sport coat open, his red tie lolling like a tongue in the heat. The man jerked the door open, and glass pieces fell onto the seat and floorboard where they reflected the sun like diamonds. The door panel was missing and there was no window crank. A woman in a white sundress and sandals ran up, running slewfoot the way some women do, holding a quilt against her chest. She spread the quilt out beside the truck and helped the man lift the boy and ease him onto the quilt. In the field behind the boy's truck, the Brahma bull bucked up white clouds of dust and barbed wire twanged like a pedal steel guitar. Above the boy's head, the sun shone brightly on the painted bee, on the bright gold word, STINGER. The sun also shone on the kid's dark hair that stuck up in points, fine as a baby's hair. Below his left shirtsleeve, above his elbow, two gashes looked deep, almost-black blood oozing steadily out. The woman brushed small triangles and rectangles of glass off his arms and finger-painted him red from his elbows to his hands.

"Where do you hurt, son?" the man in the red tie asked.

The kid's mouth twitched; his boy's eyes fluttered but didn't open. I already knew they were brown, like mine. I ran my eyes over him; there was no damage I could see but the cuts on his arm and a purple dent like a cleft in his chin. He was breathing hard, and pink, foamy spit came out onto his lips.

"They wouldn't let me in," he said, blowing bloody spit. "Dammit," his shoulders shook and tears streaked his cheeks, "they wouldn't let me in."

I don't think I've ever been as scared. I tried to bring my anger back, to force the fear away. You were wrong, I thought. My father was right. My father was in his lane; he obeyed the signs. Why didn't you slow down? I ached with hatred for that boy, and I ached with fear that he might die.

My father hadn't spoken. On the balls of his feet he leaned over the kneeling woman who held the quilt against the boy's heaving chest. The boy's eyes jerked open as a doll's do when you snatch it up.

"They wouldn't let me in," he yelled. His injuries hadn't weakened his voice or his anger.

My father leaned his face out over the boy's open eyes, as if he were showing himself, seeing whether the boy could pick him from a police line-up.

And then the police were there, the flashing red light of their squad car barely visible in the brightness of the morning. One policeman, a nameplate over his pocket read "R. Gonzales," squatted and told the boy an ambulance was on the way, while the other, "A. Hooks," used a long flashlight like a whisk broom and motioned people away. "Go on, folks, this isn't your business. Go on where you got to go. Clear the area."

My father nodded. I followed him to our car. We got in and he started the engine and we sat there listening to the steady clatter of what I knew must be a valve lifter sticking. He looked in his mirror and eased down the shoulder onto the road. Then he slowed and pulled off again. He turned off the engine. We'd gone about half a mile farther from the wreck, but he didn't back up. He opened the door and got out and started walking back. I caught up and we matched steps, our shoes slapping the pavement. An ambulance had arrived, and while we kept walking, it drove past us headed into town, siren wailing.

"It's me--I'm the one," my father told the policeman, A. Hooks, who'd shooed people away. "I'm the one he was talking about."

Hooks was writing on a clipboard. He didn't look up. "A one-vehicle accident. That's what we got here. Failure to observe warning signs. I've got all the witnesses I need."

The sun was bright behind my father's head, and his face was just a dark shape.

"Do you know where they took him?" he asked.

"Beats me. It was Suburban Ambulance Service. Ask them."

"Was he dead?" I asked.

Hooks lowered his clipboard and gave me a hard look. "I'm writing up one fatality on this report," he said. I looked at my father, whose face seemed to have gone white, though it may have been the sun. "That bull over yonder." The policeman pointed with his pencil. There, behind the downed fence posts, lay the Brahma bull, like an outcropping of limestone. "Barbed wire wrapped tighter'n hell around his neck, he went crazy trying to pull free. Tore himself up so bad he's lying there bleeding to death. Bastard'll be dead, time I find out who owns him."

The dying bull wasn't moving or making a sound. He looked like part of the natural landscape. My father and I turned and walked back to our station wagon. The only sounds were our steps on the gravel shoulder and two or three cars that blew past. Later, I thought I should have touched my father, squeezed his arm or punched it or put my hand in the small of his back or patted his shoulder the way I'd seen him pat the shoulder of a customer. If I'd thought about it at the time, I don't know if I would have done it, and if I had, I don't know if it would have made a difference. But I didn't think about it. I thought about the Brahma bull bleeding to death on the sun-bleached ground and tried to remember where I'd read that Brahmas had been brought to Texas from India because they could stand the heat. *If you can't stand the heat,* my father often said, *get out of the kitchen.*

What did we do next? We went on into town and picked up two sets of house shutters. While we were at the builder's supply, my father bought a three-eighths-inch power drill and a masonry bit, screws, and lead anchors. I missed homeroom and first period but got to school in time for my math test. My best stuff was history, literature, geography-- classes like that. The test was plane geometry. I wrote a proof my teacher later read to the class and said he was going to save. I remember, I made an A.

When I got home from school, my father wasn't there. By four-thirty, when my mother got home from the library, he still wasn't home. She'd brought me four new books: *The Voice of the Coyote,* by J. Frank Dobie; *The Rise and Fall of Jessie James,* by Robertus Love; *All About the Weather,* by Ivan Ray Tannehill; and *Profiles in Courage,* by John F. Kennedy. I helped her cook supper and we talked. She asked me about my test and I said I thought I did fine. Then I told her we'd seen a wreck that morning. I said the boy in the pickup was driving too fast and went out of control.

"Was he hurt?" she asked.

"No. A little maybe. The police took care of everything. They took him off in an ambulance, but he wasn't hurt bad." I hoped I was telling the truth.

"An ambulance." She shook her head. "God grant strength to his mother," she said so softly I wasn't sure if she was speaking to me or whispering a prayer.

The station wagon pulled into the carport just as I was putting a bowl of black-eyed peas on the table. My father came into the kitchen and squeezed the back of my neck and kissed my mother's cheek.

When we sat down to eat, she asked him about the accident. He'd just put a bite of meat into his mouth. He sat still a moment and looked at me over his fork. For the first time all afternoon, I heard the steady motor of the refrigerator. He shook his head and chewed. Then he took a drink of iced tea.

"Told you about that, did he?" He smiled at me, not a good smile.

"He said the driver was about his age. He said you all saw it happen, saw them take him away in an ambulance."

"Ambulance," my father repeated. The refrigerator shuddered and stopped, the motor cycling. The kitchen was so quiet I heard an ice cube settle in my glass of tea.

"He wasn't really hurt," I said.

"He knocked down a fence and drove into a *concrete* bridge," she said, whispering the word concrete.

"Well," my father put a forkful of peas into his mouth and chewed, "there's not much more to report." He looked at me, but spoke to my mother. "I wouldn't worry about it."

She hunched her shoulders up as if she were chilled. "It's just the sort of thing I do worry about," she said. She touched my arm and looked me in the eyes, "I worry about something happening to *you*. I guess I'll worry till I die."

"I guess you will," my father said, and none of us talked the rest of the meal.

The following Sunday was Easter, and we all went to early worship. After Sunday school, my mother wanted to ride up into the hill country to see the wildflowers in bloom. We took Highway 281 north toward Blanco and turned off onto a winding Ranch Road and saw bluebonnets and Indian paintbrush. We got back to town in time for a late lunch at Luby's Cafeteria. When we got home, my father and I put the shutters up. It was an easy job. My father said the new drill was *a real beaut.* He whistled while he worked, his song silenced by the whine of the drill, his lips pursed as if patiently offering a kiss. When we finished, we walked down to the street and looked back at the house, and he said, "You'll never miss this house, now, Son. Spot it a mile away. Find it in the dark."

The rest of the day, he holed up at the kitchen table figuring income taxes. My mother and I watched the Sunday afternoon TV movie, *The Man in the Iron Mask* with Joan Bennett and Louis Hayward, who plays Louis XIV's twin brother, kept in an iron mask so no one will see his face. Then we read until dark. I started *The Rise and Fall of Jessie James;* she was reading a book by Ring Lardner called *The Love Nest and Other Stories.*

Wier

My mother and I ate supper on TV trays in the den so my father wouldn't have to move his stacks of bills and receipts. After supper she took him a cup of coffee and asked how it was going and he said not too good. The audience on Ed Sullivan laughed, and then my father said, "None of this adds up right." My mother said something back, though I couldn't make out her words. "Damned if I will," he said.

I went to the kitchen and got an apple, and he glared at me. His face was red and he shook his head. My mother twisted a cup towel between her hands. I bit into my apple and tried to think of something to say, some way to shift their attention, but he said they had things to discuss and would I please go back into the den. I closed the door behind me and stood there a minute, holding my apple in the air, listening.

"Our income," my mother said, "doesn't live up to your ideas."

"For Christ's sake, Alice," he yelled, "the drill was marked-down. I got the shutters for nothing."

It was not the first time money talk had led to a fight between them and wouldn't be the last. I sat in front of the television and tried not to listen. My father got louder, then something banged--his fist against the table or my mother slamming a cabinet door. She came out of the kitchen and hurried through the den. She closed their bedroom door behind her, and the house was so quiet I turned down the TV. An hour later, my father came out of the kitchen and went back to the bedroom. Soon, my mother appeared in the gray light of the television, clutching sheets and a quilt.

She took the back cushions off the couch, and I helped her tuck a sheet over the seat cushions. The quilt was one my grandmother--my father's mother--made before she died. I have wondered since whether my mother was thinking about the quilt's pattern, a design of interlocking circles called "wedding ring." It was soft and clean and smelled of the cedar chest where my mother stored keepsakes.

A bed on a couch may be a discomfort to some, but is always inviting to me--a holiday night and out-of-town company, awake in the den with only the glowing light of the TV, the rest of the house quiet with sleep--cozy and special (like a secret, somehow). I think my mother felt that way, too, because she fixed hot chocolate, and we sat there on the bed we'd made so she could lie down in anger, and she smiled.

"I'm just cutting off my nose to spite my face," she said. "This is no punishment for your father. He's probably already sawing logs, spread out across our bed." She moved her hand over the quilt, palm down,

14

around and around, following the tracks of stitches. She sipped from her cup, her eyes shiny from tears or from the heat coming up off the milk.

I drank my hot chocolate, hiding behind the cup.

"Nothing bothers him," she said. "As soon as his head hits the pillow, he's asleep. Clear conscience, I guess, but sometimes it makes me so mad." Her teeth bright blue in the television light, she smiled while she complained--as if my father's ability to sleep regardless of calamity were secretly prideful to her. "I wish I were more like him," she said. "I wish you were," she whispered.

She waited for me to say something, but I only nodded.

"I've already forgiven him," she said. "You want to sleep here tonight?"

"Sure," I said.

I lay there in the dark and watched the ten-o'clock news, watching as I had each evening since it happened, for a report of the wreck. There had been a shooting, a wife had discovered her husband with another woman. The wife stared at me from the television screen, shaking her head back and forth, *no, no,* and when two Bexar county deputies took her by the arms, her body went stiff and they had to carry her. Her husband, who was expected to recover, was shown lying on a stretcher, his body a white mound. As they slid him into an ambulance, he smiled and waved. After the weather report--continued heat and drouth, no relief in sight--I turned the television off.

I'd searched the pages of the San Antonio *Light,* read all the stories printed since the accident. A smallish headline, EASTER MIRACLE, had caught my eye that morning: the music minister and the choir director of the Trinity Baptist Church, returning from a conference in Houston, had walked away with only scratches when their single-engine Cessna hit a power line and came down in a field of maize east of San Antonio.

The day the wreck happened, during lunch period at school I'd gone to the pay phone by the Coke machine and called the Suburban Ambulance Service; then, starting with the Medical and Surgical Memorial where I was born, phoned every hospital in the yellow pages. There was no record of an accident on the Poteet Highway. No news had to mean that the boy had not been seriously injured and that the death of one Brahma bull, even in unusual circumstances, did not warrant public notice.

For a while, I saw the cop in his dark uniform as a priest hearing my father's confession and absolving him with the sacrificial Brahma bull. Later, I realized I was seeking my own absolution. It seems to me, God gives us rules to keep, then sets us up to break them. I've wondered why: so we'll feel guilty? so we'll ask forgiveness? so we'll need Him? I've wondered if that boy did die but, somehow, it never got reported. I've wondered if he ever forgot the singing barbed wire and the impact of concrete and if he still drives recklessly. I've wondered how often, in the past thirty years, he's met a station wagon in traffic and looked for my father's face, for my face, behind the windshield.

I picture a man, old as I am, beside me at a light, both our engines idling. He's in a dented black pickup, a painted-gold bumblebee and STINGER no longer bright-shining but still visible on the truck's side. He turns, and the boy's face stares at me from behind a mask of middle-age.

I've wondered if the face of Louis XIV's twin brother, the face behind the iron mask, mirrored the slow, daily changes in the king's face. I recall looking down at my father's face in his casket. That face--fixed smile, tiny veins like cracks in a fleshy nose, hair gray where a stranger had brushed it back from the temples--is the face I now see staring back at me from my medicine-cabinet mirror. I've wondered about the sins of the father being visited upon the son, wondered what those sins might include.

What I finally decided is this: that moment in the bright sun on the side of the highway was not my father's moment--it was mine. Whatever would have made my father stay awake at night, as unable to sleep as I was lying under my grandmother's wedding-ring quilt, had happened to him long ago, if at all. I don't know whether he ever stared into a face with blood on its lips and hurt in its eyes and saw himself staring back. I know what losses I recognized when I looked into the wounded face of a boy still innocent enough not to slow down, still guiltless enough to be angry, not scared. What I saw was my own defiant face, the way I used to be, without shame, before that moment happened to me.

Returnings

Elaine thought that hard work might clear her head, might not let her thoughts turn to her son. She had been coaxing the tractor through the field for four hours, turning two hundred acres into corduroy. When the rusting International was dead center in the farm, it began to miss and sputter, giving up under the April sun, far from the tractor shed. Elaine reached around the steering wheel, pulling the choke out a bit, hoping the carburetor would pass the water that she knew was in the gasoline, remembering with a pang that she had not drained the little glass water trap under the fuel tank. She hoped that her husband had been wrong when he'd told her that middle-aged women couldn't farm. Yet she had forgotten to get the water out of the line on a tractor that had been sitting up three months, its gas tank sweating on the inside. She frowned at the coughing machine. They were supposed to buy a brand new tractor that year, a 1967 model. But there was no longer any need.

The engine fluttered and died. She checked her watch and saw that it was eleven o'clock. Climbing down she poured a drink of water from a thermos tied under the metal seat with a strand of twine. She turned to stare at her house nearly a mile away, satisfied at the even rows of brown dirt she had heaped up.

She was a nurturer and felt that this quality, better than any man's mechanical ability, would help her bring life to the fields of her farm. In her blood was a fondness for generation more powerful than muscle and bone. The fondness would make her a farmer.

Elaine hoped that her husband would see that the tractor had stalled out and would bring her some tools. His back was hurting, and he had little to do but watch out the kitchen window or endure Lyndon Johnson on television talking about the war. A half hour after the engine died she saw his green truck bobbing toward her very slowly across the unplowed portion of field.

"Either you're out of gas or the engine sucked up a charge of water," he said, handing her a small tool box through the truck window. He was tanned, clean-shaven and looked strong, but he winced when he raised the box up to her hands.

"Stay in the truck," she said.

"I plan to. The ride out here's awful rough." He ran his hand through his dark, graying curls. "You know what to do?" He asked in a way which pleaded that she did.

"Yes. I've got plenty gas. It's water, I'm sure. You stay put." She fixed him with a worried stare and plucked at the checked cotton blouse that clung to her with sweat.

Her husband blinked and rested his forearms on top of the steering wheel. "I'm sorry that you've got to do this. I'll be better in a month or so."

She gave him a smile as she pulled a pair of slip-joint pliers from the box. "Joe told me how to do this. I suppose you taught him somewhere along the line."

His eyes scanned the farm. "It's amazing how much he did around here."

Elaine did not answer. There was nothing to say that they did not already feel in their blood and would always feel about an eighteen-year-old son who was healthy one week, plowing and fixing things, and dead the next from encephalitis. They refused to reminisce, but they talked around their son at mealtime, as though he were at the table and they were ignoring him. When they touched in any way, the message of him was on their skins, and they knew their loss. Talking could not encompass what had gone from them.

They had brought up two girls, now married and raising families in other towns, good girls who visited. But is was to be Joe's farm.

She made a face as she pulled the bowl of the water trap off the fuel line, spilling cold gasoline into her hands. The smell would stay in the cracks of her skin for hours like a bad memory. Working carefully in the sun she heard the truck start and turn for the house. She took a part out of the carburetor, cleared it of water and put everything together, opening the gas valve once more only to discover a leak. Twenty minutes passed before she had the tractor ready to run. Wiping her hands, she heard at the periphery of her attention the steady chop of a helicopter in the distance, a common sound in this part of the parish because of an air training facility across the line in Mississippi. She mounted the tractor, pulled out the choke, and with a finger in the starter ring paused to look toward a helicopter which was passing closer than usual. A gunship, armed and camouflaged, skirted the edge of her field. It hovered a moment, approached with a whopping roar and finally settled down in a circular dust storm seventy yards from her. She held her straw hat over her brown hair, glad at least that the machine

18

had lit in an unplowed section. There was only one person in the glassed-in cabin, and he watched her carefully. The pilot's stare made her uneasy. She had imagined military folk to be generally on the move, having no time for meditation. There was also something unorthodox about the pilot's size. He appeared too small, his headphones seeming like cantaloupe halves clapped to his ears. He was rather dark.

After a while he kicked open a door and jumped out, the huge blades dying in speed above him. Jogging across the field in loose combat fatigues, his pistol holster flying out from his side with each leap over the bumpy soil, he trailed a partially unfolded map. Elaine squinted and saw that he was Oriental and very young, maybe twenty.

"Hello," he said, smiling mightily. "Can you be of assistance?"

She glanced at the helicopter, wondering briefly if he had somehow stolen it. "What's wrong? You have engine trouble too?" she asked, pointing down at the tractor.

"No, no," he said, smiling so that his face seemed ready to split. He appeared desperately afraid that she would fear him. "I need advice."

She could see behind his smile and climbed down to the ground next to him. He was the size of a boy, his features rounded and new. "Advice about what?"

"It is hard for me to ask," he said, backing away, tilting his head to the left, to the right, almost crying though his grin. "I am lost." He began unfolding a map, placing it on the ground. "If you please could tell me where I am, I could get back to base. I am on my solo training flight and have hour to return."

She stooped and tried to study the map, but it contained no red-lined highways and town names like the filling station maps she was used to. It was lettered in a bizarre military code. She told him she could not make heads or tails of it. She was intelligent, and her father had sent her to college for two years, but she could not deal with a map that didn't have Poireauville or Leroux spelled out on it. "I know where the fort is over the line in Mississippi, but I couldn't tell you how to fly there. Why don't we just give them a call and have an instructor come out to fly you back?"

"No," he wailed, his smile collapsing at last. At once she thought of the pinched faces she saw on the newscasts in the evenings, the small people running from thatched houses, pillars of smoke in the background, the rattle of weapons. "If I fail at pilot school, I get sent back to Vietnam as foot soldier." He turned to look longingly on his machine as though already it had been taken from him.

She stood and leaned against her tractor. "Your instructor would give you another chance, wouldn't he?"

He shook his head vigorously. "My instructor wants to see me dead in a rice paddy. He is a big American with red hair. Every day he tells me, 'Le Ton, if you do not fly right we send you home with a cheap rifle to fight VC.'"

She studied him a while, looked back to the farmhouse and then to the map. Her husband could not read it, she knew. Joe probably could have.

"Le Ton. Is that you name?"

"Yes. I am from farmland too." He folded up his map.

"You flew out of Fort Exter?" The more she looked at him the younger he appeared, some mother's favorite, she guessed, noticing the good nature in his eyes. Why else would he be trying so hard to stay alive?

"That is so. I fly by map and directions given by my instructor at base. No radio." His face darkened. "My instructor gives me bad directions."

"You have an hour left to get back?"

He nodded. "Thank you for trying to help me."

She wiped her palms on her jeans. "I'll tell you what, son. I can't judge anything from that map, but if you take me up in that machine of yours, I might be able to show you where the fort is, and then you could drop me back off here. I don't think it's more than thirty miles or so." She could hardly believe what she'd said. She might be doing something illegal or unpatriotic.

He took to the idea instantly. "Ah, that would be good. I fly you a few miles outside of base and return here. Plenty time to get back to base." She hung her straw hat on the breather pipe of the tractor and stepped over the big unplowed clods of earth to the gunship, climbing in next to him as he flipped overhead switches, manipulated foot pedals and lifted hand levers at his side. The craft surged and vibrated like a tool shed in a tornado. In a moment they were whanging through the sky.

"Go east," she yelled. Elaine watched for the water tower in Poireauville but could hardly keep her eyes off the running fields below her, the sugarcane roads, bayous, levees and willow brakes which flew by as in a dream or a wide-screened movie at a world's fair. It was difficult to concentrate on any landmark when the giant oaks and longleaf pines were sailing just a few feet below. Le Ton glanced at her for direction. The water tower she saw in the distance had to be Poireauville's, and she pointed toward it, but when the craft came within two miles of the round silver tank, she felt disoriented and panicky. It was too small to be Poireauville's, too freshly painted. Le Ton flew a wide circle around it and she wished that all little towns still painted their names on the tanks as they did when she was a child.

"Which way?" he asked.

She scanned the ground. There were too many trees. Poireauville was a cut-over hamlet and did not support such a welter of sycamores. Perhaps they had veered a few miles northeast and were over Rodeaux. Looking to her left, she spotted a set of smokestacks and suddenly wished her husband were with her. An area man could look at a smokestack from three miles and tell the name of the settlement, the type of mill, the owner of the machinery and the names of his children. But she was lost.

She spotted a rusty thread of railroad and pointed down to it. "That's the Missouri Pacific branch line. Follow it." Her son had loved railroads and had shown her maps of the state's lines enough times that she had a vague notion of where the local tracks went. Before he was old enough to drive, she would take him on long rides so he could take pictures of stations and engines. She remembered telling him that he should photograph people, not only objects. People are what have to be remembered. She looked down at an abandoned crossroads grocery, its windows boarded up. Places are nothing.

Le Ton swirled above the railroad for six miles, looking down and then checking his compass. "Lady, we fly north? You are sure of the railroad?" He had lost his smile completely. His face shone with a nervous sweat. It worried her that he was more frightened than she was. Looking down, she thought that perhaps this was the old north track instead of the branch which led east. Everywhere were oaks and occasionally a flat field of sugarcane she did not recognize. She saw a barn she had never seen before, a large white home and two rows of tenant houses. She felt like a child lost in a thousand acres of razor-leafed cane.

"Go that way," she yelled, pointing to her right. Studying the ground she saw a cornfield slip under her and a tenant house which seemed to be empty, its iron roof bloody with rust. She was looking for a laundry line full of drying clothes which would tell the presence of a woman. A full laundry line behind a house where the truck was gone would be a lucky find. She did not want to risk landing in the yard of a stiff-necked sharecropper who would call the sheriff before he heard her out.

A weathered cypress house passed below, and she asked Le Ton for field glasses, which he produced from a rack under his seat. She focused on the back yard. A string of laundry danced on the line, but there were many cumberstone checkered shirts, and in the front yard, two trucks.

A mile-and-a-half across the field was a poorer house, the chimney broken at the top, the roof swaybacked. She motioned to it when she saw in its back yard the wink of towels and sheets. She thought back to the days when she still hung out the wash, the clean damp smell of the pillow cases, and the breezy mornings her son chased his sisters through the laundry, the bright cotton licking their faces.

Le Ton was shouting, "The house is behind. Keep going?"

Looking back with the glasses she saw no car and no electric meter on the wires leading along the side of the house. "Put down in the field across the road from that shack." There was no need to soil the laundry.

The helicopter descended slowly into a pasture as several bony, fly-bitten cows lurched away into a grove of wild plum trees. As the craft touched down, she looked across the gravel road to a porch where a stout black woman sat in a rocker and shaded her eyes.

Le Ton stopped the engine. "Why do we stop here?" He looked around at the sickly fields and the paintless tenant shack.

"I've got to ask directions from somebody who won't call a newspaper." She jumped to the ground and he followed her to the road where she instructed him to wait.

Once on the porch she sidestepped a gap in the flooring.

"Don't bust a leg," the black woman sang, touching the kerchief that bound her hair. "My man's supposed to fix that when he can find a right board."

"How you doing? I'm Elaine Campbell from down in Burkhalter community. Do you know where that is?"

The other woman stood, adjusted her apron and stared at the floor. "No, ma'am," she said. "Don't you?"

"Well of course I know where it is when I'm there. But this boy and I seem to be lost."

The black woman looked across the road at Le Ton who stood like a frail post against the slack barbed wire. "How come you ain't got on your uniform?"

"I'm not in the army. He is. He got lost over my place in Burkhalter and I was trying to show him the way to Fort Exter when we got lost again."

"I don't know where Burkhalter is."

"It's not far from Poireauville."

"Law." She sat down. "That's twenty miles off with the crow. The roads don't hardly run thataway." She peered across the gravel lane again. "They let that little Chinaman run that big machine?"

Elaine turned, looked at Le Ton and grinned. "He's on a training mission. If they find out at the fort that he got lost, they'll send him back to Vietnam as a foot soldier. I'm just trying to help him out."

"Vietnam," the other woman repeated. "I heard that word a lot. My onliest boy been sent over there. I got three girls, but only one boy. He use to be at Exter too. Name's Vergil Bankston."

Elaine sat in a straight-back chair and motioned for Le Ton to cross the road.

As he walked up to the porch, Mary Bankston examined him, then let out a gentle, high-pitched whine. "If he ain't just a baby, though. Is all Vietnam peoples easy lost like you?"

Le Ton smiled defensively, considering the question a long time. He sat on the porch floor between the women, facing them, and folded his legs. "I am stupid to Americans. Most trainees are farm people. We know how to plow with ox, how to use hoe." He made a little hoeing movement with his arms. "It is very hard to learn vectors and compression ratios, how to make big fast helicopters run right." He looked from one woman's face to the other searching for understanding. "My cousin, Tak Dok came to fly Corsair airplanes. In training flight his cockpit shield blows off and he radios back what happens. Man in the tower says land at once. Tak Dok brings his plane down in the field of corn and lands without much damage. Instructors send him back to be foot soldier because they mean for him to come back to his airfield to land at once." He looked over his shoulder toward his craft. "Last month Tak Dok is killed. My young cousin was a good pilot but could not always understand your way with words."

Mary Bankston passed a long mother's look to Elaine, the expression a woman owns at night when she sits up listening to a child cough and rattle, knowing there is nothing she can do but act out of her best feelings. "I got a pot of hot water on the stove. I can drip coffee in a minute." She smiled at Le Ton. "Got a teabag somewhere, too."

"We don't have a whole lot of time," Elaine said, looking down on Le Ton's camouflage cap. She pulled it off a moment to look at the thick, close-cropped hair and the young brassy skin at the roots. Everything about him was small and young, laden with possibilities. "Do you have any idea how far we are from the Mississippi line?"

"You wants to go to Exter, don't you?"

"Yes."

"Then tell him to fly straight east to that brand new interstate about thirty miles, then take a right and follow it down to that big green sign what says Fort Exter."

Elaine placed her left palm on her forehead. "I should have remembered that. I've never been on it, but I knew it was there."

"Sure enough," Mary Bankston said. "Even a farmer Chinaman can find a four-lane highway. I been on it twice to go see Vergil."

Elaine returned Le Ton's cap. "Didn't you pass over that interstate to get into this region?"

He thought about this for a moment, and then with the expression of an old man wise to betrayal, he answered her. "Instructor says fly over Gulf and then come inland."

"Nice guy. Let's go, then." Mary Bankston offered to let them have two fried apple pies for their trip, but they declined.

"He ain't never going to get no bigger if he don't eat," she yelled after them as they crossed the fence.

Elaine called back. "Don't tell anybody about us, especially your son."

She nodded from her paintless porch. "Who gonna believe me?"

Le Ton started the engine and the big gunship whirled off into the sky. She looked below and saw the old railroad they had followed earlier. "Why aren't you heading east? You could let me off on a highway outside of base, and I could figure a way to get home."

"That would not be right," he said. "You have been too helpful. I should not put you out in the middle of a wilderness." He glanced back to the tenant house where Mary Bankston was probably watching him as she would a young child crossing the street. "I also have been on the big highway the black lady speaks of. I did not know it ran north-south. It is not on the map the instructor gives me."

With the field glasses she found the correct water tower, a larger structure to the south emblazoned with "Seniors '66," a spray paint legend her son had helped create one moonless night. She remembered how Sammy, the local deputy, had caught him, bringing him to the house, revealing what her son had done, working a wink into his speech while Joe stood behind him in the front door, repentant and fearful.

She had never told her husband. He wouldn't have punished their son severely, but Elaine let her instinct to protect overpower her need to discipline. Now as the painted words swam in the field glasses, she couldn't say whether she would ever tell her husband. She forced her eyes away, over to the highway, and in a minute found the blacktop that crawled to her farm. She had no idea that the place appeared so drowsy, the roofs tired with rust, the crystal green ponds oval like the sleepy eyes of children. Le Ton circled to the rear of the farm to avoid buzzing the house and set down where he had earlier.

"I hope your tractor starts now," he said, breaking into an easy smile.

She reached over and grabbed his neck, kissing him on the cheek. "Call Ralph Campbell in Poireauville exchange and tell me how you did," she said.

He was surprised, but he nodded in a way that showed he understood. After seeing her jump down and clear the blades, he gave her a broad wave, then mounted the sky.

She watched until the craft disappeared over a distant neighboring farmhouse, the home of John Thompson whose blonde daughter had loved her son. She listened to the clamor of the machine pounding into the eastern sky.

When she turned, she noticed her husband's truck lurching out toward her. Quickly she reached under the tank and turned off the gasoline valve. He arrived, getting out this time, holding his back and walking over like someone much older. She held her breath, then asked the question. "What brings you out here?"

"I been sleeping," he said, rubbing his smooth jaw. "Something woke me up. I just looked out and saw you still hadn't started the tractor." He gave her a questioning look. "Why didn't you walk in and get me?"

"How's your back?"

He straightened up slowly, as if to test himself. "Feels better this afternoon."

"That's good. No, I've taken everything apart and blown out the water. It just won't start."

He walked up to the controls, pulled the starter ring twice and listened. He reached up under the tank. "You forgot to reopen the gas line," he said.

25

She kicked at a clod of dirt. "I can't believe I forgot that."

"Women farmers," he said, smiling that cool, wrinkled smile of his.

"I suppose you've never done the same."

He thought a bit. "One morning I tried and tried to start this thing. I ran down the battery before Joe, he was about nine then, came out to the shed and turned on the gas for me. He said, "Daddy, what would you ever do without me?""

She walked over and stood next to him, the skin on her arms prickling. The empty quiet of the field was oppressive, and she pulled the starter ring. The tractor chuckled alive, but as soon as it did he reached over and pushed the kill switch, the quiet settling on them like a memory. "We've got to get away for awhile," he said, his voice so shaky it scared her. "Leave the tractor here. Let's get cleaned up and drive into town." He glanced up into the sky. "Let's drive two towns over and get a fancy meal. You need it. You never get off this place." He pounded the dull red tractor once with a fist.

She looked at the eastern horizon, then put her arm easily around his back and hugged him, her freckled cheek pressing against the fresh khaki of his shirt. Slipping a hand up to the hot skin of his neck, she felt his blood coursing away, knowing it to be her blood as well. They stood together in the half-plowed field, in the middle of all they had lost. He took her hand, leading her to the passenger door of the truck, opening it for her as if they were on a date.

An hour later she was clipping small gold circles to her earlobes, and her husband was shaving. In the den the telephone began its slow rattle, and she bolted past the bathroom door for it. At first she was afraid to pick it up.

"Yes?" she answered. "I see. Yes." Her expression remained neutral. "I understand you perfectly. Sure. And thank you for calling." She replaced the receiver and could not keep herself from smiling.

They got into the shimmering sedan and drove out onto the unlined road, heading through the hot afternoon toward town. In a month the land around her would bear cornstalks growing like children. She cast a long admiring gaze at the field she'd been plowing, at the straightness of her rows where they glimmered under the sun, rails of dirt running east under a safe and empty sky.

Rise

Tom Franklin

Lyle rose early and made coffee. He stood over the stove sipping and staring out the window, where it was still dark. He could make out the dim lines of Evelyn's car, and of his truck beside the gate, and he knew Mace would be sleeping in the cab, drunk. He'd heard somebody drop him off last night, the dogs howling, the truck door slam. Finishing his coffee, he rinsed the cup and left it hanging on its peg by the kniferack and went to put on his boots.

He locked the door behind him and buttoned his jacket up to his neck. His breath curled away in the wind as he went down the porch steps with his hands jammed in his pockets and hurried across the slippery frozen grass to the truck. The windshield was frosted, solid ice. When he opened the door a cowboy hat rolled out. Smell of beer. Lyle mumbling picked up the hat and shook it off and looked at Mace in his big sheepskin coat, the heavy collar hiding all but the long black hair, his knees nothing but frayed white holes. He was trembling so hard you could hear his teeth.

"Wake up, you bum," Lyle said, swatting him with the cowboy hat.

Mace shifted, coughed.

Lyle reached in and moved Mace's feet, the boot leather icy, then he climbed in and ground the starter until the truck kicked to life. He raced the engine, the mirrors filling up white with exhaust fumes.

"Wake up, boy," he said. "Get your goddamn feet off me."

Mace squinted over his collar. "Cold," he said.

Lyle turned on the wipers, watched them rasp across the ice.

Mace sat up and rubbed his eyes. "What time is it?"

"Bout four."

"Shit, why so early?"

Mace picked up the cowboy hat and squared it on his head. He leaned and turned the rear view mirror and looked at himself then turned it back, nowhere near where it was. "God almighty," he said, "I look like I was sent for and couldn't come and when I got there I wasn't needed."

Lyle adjusted the mirror.

"I ain't drunk." Mace took the hat off. "Okay, a little, maybe. Who can blame me."

"How come you didn't come on in the house?"

"I seen Evelyn's car."

Lyle shrugged. "You coulda came on in."

"Yall make up?" Mace asked.

"You might say."

"Get you any?"

Lyle looked at him.

"Whoa ho," Mace sang, "the boy done got his tree trimmed."

"Where'd you go last night?" Lyle asked.

"Highway 43 Club. Me and Hobart and them. Played a little pool, drunk a little beer, did some dancin. Won me this hat off somebody playin quarters."

"What time'd you get back?"

"I don't know, couple hours ago. Old Clemmons dropped me off."

By now Lyle could see and he rattled the gear and they eased past the mailbox into the road.

"Think you might pull over get me some coffee?" Mace asked.

"I reckon."

They stopped at the store and with the truck idling hurried across the concrete slab past the diesel tanks where a Peterbilt sat humming, its lights off.

"That Evan's rig?" Mace asked.

"Naw, that's Juicy's."

They went into the store. Hurley sat behind the counter reading the paper. He looked at them over his glasses then looked back at the paper. A cigarette lay smoking in the ashtray at his elbow and he lifted it to his lips and its end glowed bright orange and he returned it to the ashtray and turned the pages of the paper.

Lyle went to the machine and poured himself a large cup of black coffee. He rubbed the stubble on his chin and neck and ran a finger into his ear. Mace with a slight reel to his walk went down the candy aisle to the men's room. Lyle stepped over to the magazine rack and looked across the faces of the starlets there. In a minute Mace came out of the back with his hair in a ponytail and his shirt tucked in. He stopped at the coffee maker then met Lyle at the counter. Hurley, the paper rattling, stood and came over and punched keys on the register.

"One-fifty," he said.

Lyle and Mace fished in their pants pockets, coming out with the exact change. Lyle held the door for Mace and they went out sipping at their smoking cups.

In the truck Mace put his cowboy hat on his knee and fiddled with the heater knobs. "My feet's like ice," he said. "Can't feel my toes." He lifted his foot for Lyle to see.

"Them steel toes?"

"Yeah."

"Hell, no wonder."

"We gettin Jimmyboy?"

"Got to."

"How come?"

"He's got the gun."

There was little traffic on the causeway and Lyle drove in silence. He shook a cigarette from his pack and offered the pack to Mace. Mace got one with shaky fingers and lit it with the truck's lighter, then lit Lyle's. They smoked and looked out their windows at the gas stations just opening for the day and at the bait shops that never closed. A few blacks were already fishing along the rails of the bridges, coathoods up and bursts of breath issuing from them like morse code. In the distance the smokestacks from the paper mill blinked warnings against low-flying aircraft.

After awhile Mace cleared his throat. "She gonna stay this time?"

"Don't know."

"She say when she's leavin?"

Lyle shook his head.

"Try not to talk so much," Mace said. "Fella gets his tree trimmed you think he'd feel like tellin his buddy the details. Specially when that buddy ain't had none in lord knows how long."

"Nothin to tell."

Mace rolled down his window and let his ashes fly then closed the window. "Jeez Louise it is *cold*."

They crossed the bridge with the river underneath and the mill to their right and rode down the hill into Prichard. There were condemned buildings, and paralleling the highway were railroad tracks with strings of empty box cars. The ones with closed doors would have transients sleeping in them. Lyle turned left and they crossed the tracks.

"Where's Jimmyboy livin these days anyhow?" Mace asked.

"Right up here."

They entered a trailer park with rusty cars in every yard and sleepy-looking dogs emerging from under the trailers barking halfhearted steam. Behind a seedy double-wide Lyle saw three blacks standing

29

around a smoking barrel, stamping their feet and passing back and forth between them a fifth in a paper bag.

The names of the oyster shell streets were Biblical: Matthew, Mark, Luke, John. Lyle put his cigarette in his mouth and turned left onto John. Jimmyboy lived at the end of the road, in the trailer of some woman he'd taken up with.

"I don't see no lights," Mace said.

They left the truck chugging and got out and hurried across the dirt yard. On the steps they both pounded on the door, a draft reaching up at them from under the trailer and stinging their dry legs.

"Wake up you dickweed," Mace said through his teeth.

A light flared in the rear of the trailer then disappeared, like somebody waving a flashlight. They heard footsteps down the hall and in a minute Jimmyboy's dark frown appeared in the window.

"Hold on," he said.

The handle rattled and the door swung in, Jimmyboy holding the flashlight, standing behind it with an army blanket on his bony shoulders. They brushed past him and stood in a tight circle in the dark room and Jimmyboy closed the door and shined the light in their eyes. Mace shielded his face and Jimmyboy let the lantern drop.

"Where's your fuckin lights?" Mace asked.

"Storm come through while ago," Jimmyboy said. "Knocked the juice out."

"You ready?" Lyle asked.

"Naw man, I ain't goin."

"The hell you mean you ain't goin?"

"My old lady, she say it ain't right, what yall fixin to do."

"What *we* fixin to do," Mace said.

"What's this we shit, paleface?" Jimmyboy said. He turned off the flashlight.

"Bull shit," Mace said. "You're goin if I have to drag your skinny black ass out the fuckin door."

"Jesus," Lyle said. "Well did you get the gun at least?"

"Man you not serious?"

A noise from the back of the trailer silenced them.

"Jimmyboy?"

"It's okay Momma," he called.

"Jimmyboy?"

"Man yall got to go," he whispered. "Albertha find out who I'm talkin to she'll get her razor."

"*Jimmyboy?*"

"I'm comin Momma."

Lyle said, "Have you got the gun?"

Jimmyboy pushed it into his hands, it was heavy and warm.

"We'll see you," Lyle said.

"I ain't forgettin this," Mace told Jimmyboy.

"Like the great white elephant he never forget," Jimmyboy said. He opened the door and the cold air swirled in around their legs. Mace went out first and as Lyle followed him he felt Jimmyboy's hand on his shoulder but he didn't stop. He went down the steps after Mace and they got into the truck. It had started raining, you could see it on the windshield and past the windshield Jimmyboy standing in the door.

They sat watching and in the bedroom the curtains moved and half of Jimmyboy's old lady's face appeared in the window like some stonefaced voodoo mask until the curtains fell shut and Lyle put the truck in reverse. For an uncomfortable second the tires spun on the ice then they caught and the truck bounced over the road. They held their coffee cups and sipped at them while Lyle drove slowly past the grumbling dogs and over the oyster shells and across the railroad tracks and past the deserted buildings and boarded-up windows and rusting box cars.

The gun on the seat between them.

"Is it loaded?" Lyle asked.

Mace picked it up and ejected the clip then pushed it back in. "Yeah."

They rode, had each smoked another cigarette before Mace said, "You know what I just remembered?"

"Hm."

"It's Christmas Eve."

Lyle nodded.

"You think Mike realized that?"

"I don't know."

"Other day Sammy seen him in Food World," Mace said. "Said he went up to him said Howdy, Mike, how you doin? And Mike, he says, Not bad for a dead man. That's a hell of a thing to say to somebody, ain't it? You're tryin to act normal and he pulls that shit on you."

"I guess," Lyle said.

Mace was holding the pistol.

31

"Fuck, it's cold," he said.

They went back through the tunnel and over the causeway, past the fishermen and the seagulls that stood on the concrete railing or perched on the light poles. They went under the Bayway.

When they passed Argiro's Service Station Mace looked back over his shoulder. "Did you see that?"

"What?"

"That midget," he said. "He was puttin air in a tire. He wasn't even squattin down, just sorta bent over like."

Mace was turning the gun over in his hands.

They got out in Mike's yard. He lived in the woods with no neighbors for a mile and the sky seen in patches through the trees was starting to pale. The rain was gone, leaving a dewy mist in the air that stung their faces as they looked at one another across the top of the truck.

"It's good luck to see a midget," Mace said.

The line of windows across the front of Mike's house was lit, as if he'd gone from room to room turning on lights. The front door stood open.

They saw him. Through one of the windows, in one of the rooms. Walking. He appeared in another window and disappeared. Lyle reached back into the truck and got the pistol. He slipped it into his coat pocket. He took one last drag on his cigarette and dropped it into the frost. Mace did likewise. With their hands in their pockets they walked across the yard, past the frozen birdbath, past a shovel standing upright in the earth. Mike's dog came to the door and wagging its wire of a tail trotted to the edge of the porch and jumped off and came toward them. Its ears flattened as Mace bent to rub its muzzle and allow himself to be licked in the face. His and the dog's breaths mingled and Lyle waited for a minute as Mace said soft quiet words that only the dog heard. When Mace stood and they went up the steps the dog stayed in the yard.

Lyle rapped on the doorjamb but got no answer. So knocking the ice from their boots they stepped into the living room. There was no furniture, not even curtains. Mace stopped and put his red fingers into a fistmark left in the paneling. He pursed his lips.

They heard a toylike whistle from the back of the house and exchanged a glance. Mace shook his head and walked back out. Lyle watched him cross the porch and sit on the steps without looking around. The dog nosed up to him and Mace took its face in his hands.

Lyle turned and went down the hall. Cigarette butts lay on the carpet, filters smashed into black smudges. It was freezing in the house, drafty.

The whistle again.

Mike sat in his den, on a stool at the table before his model train. When there had been barbecues here, when Mike had worked at the mill with Lyle and Mace and Jimmyboy, they had stood in this room together and drunk beer and watched the train circling the tracks and there were women in the next room, you could hear their pleasant voices in the air, and outside the sound of children.

Lyle cleared his throat and Mike looked around. His left eye was sewn shut, the feeling in that side of his face gone. Lyle had heard he'd gotten something in his eye and since he couldn't feel anything he hadn't noticed it until it was too late. It was one of the things a brain tumor could do.

"Hey, Mike," Lyle said.

Mike wore his black longshoreman's coat and a stocking cap. Lyle went and stood at the corner of the table and put his fingers on the cold wood and he and Mike watched the train go around.

The table was different now.

There was dirt and grass spread across it, it had become a tiny landscape, like a section of land seen from an airplane lifting from a runway. There were rocks the size of footballs that were like mountains to the train that passed them and sped around the curved track into what became a miniature town, little buildings made of wood and cardboard. Two city blocks of two and three story buildings with tiny windows cut out and names of shops printed on signs, a barber shop with its striped pole, a Western Auto with a line of toy bicycles before it. A motorcycle parked in front of a diner. There were streets of packed dirt and stoplights and stop signs and light poles strung with fishing line and for a water tower a styrofoam cup painted gray with toothpick legs. There were tiny metal cars. A white church with its steeple and cross and beside it a little graveyard with a spiked fence. There was a forest of weeds and twigs like tiny trees between the town and mountains and beyond the mountains there were more trees.

Lyle studied the train as it passed through the town without stopping, as it went through a railroad crossing, a little red light blinking a warning. The black engine was old-timey with a smoke stack and large cow-catcher. The coal car behind it held black rocks. Its rail car hauled sticks whittled to resemble logs. There was a tank car, a box car, a passenger car. A red caboose.

"It used to be my kid's," Mike said. "He got it for Christmas one year and stopped playing with it that same day. It just sat in the box till I got it out."

Lyle watched the train and looked over the terrain, at the scale, the attention to detail. Out past the forest, on the far side of the table, the train passed a little farm, a barn and farmhouse, a silo, a windmill. A tractor. There were pens that held little pigs and cattle, there were feeders and tight balls of pine straw like bales of hay and there was a toothpick corral with tiny plastic horses, the kind you buy in a bag. Some were in a bucking position and others were calm. Inch high pewter cowboys stood around the fence, watching.

The train whistled and Lyle moved around the table for a closer look. One of the horses was blue and slightly bigger than the rest. It stood perfectly calm. Probably that was what the tiny cowboys were discussing. It must have come from the forest beyond the mountains. A traveler spotted it from the train window and word spread. A blue horse. The cowboys captured it, they chose their fastest horses and got the best roper from among them to lead the chase and they rose early one morning, before dawn, and they slipped quietly out of the barn with shouldered saddles, smoking cigarettes and laughing nervously. The blue horse would be clever, wily. It would be a dangerous chase of speed and dust and jumps and ducking of tree limbs like thick arms swatting at you as the earth rushed by. A chase that might go for miles, hours. The blue horse ahead at a full gallop, losing the cowboys one by one to fatigue or injury or death, until at last the only cowboy is the roper, a young man with short hair and a tan face, his hat beating against his shoulders, spurs bloody, a tall young man with a pretty wife at home asleep, a wife whose thighs he parted the night before, who held him knowing of his dangerous morning race, knowing he was the best roper. With her lips opened and her eyes closed as he moves over her, she is thinking of him on his horse, his head low, sweat streaming in muddy tracks down his skin. She sees the blue horse before him and his hand rising and circling and the loop materializing in the air over him like a tornado of his own creation, lashing out from his open palm at the straining musculature of the blue horse and its pounding flanks and rippling skin and settling over its neck, its flowing blue mane, its frothy nostrils and teeth, its wide glaring eyes.

Lyle slipped the gun out of his pocket and laid it gingerly on the table, at the edge of the forest.

"Gotta go," he said. "We're gonna be late for work."

Mace and the dog were in the truck waiting. The dog sat between them on the seat. When Lyle shut his door the dog got up and turned nervous circles until Mace made it lie down and put its head in his lap. "Shhhh," he said. Lyle lit his last cigarette, and smoking it drove through the woods and out to the highway and got onto the causeway. The early morning traffic was thickening, cars headed to work were starting to turn off their lights.

Mace hugged himself. "Don't your heater work?"

They took a right and got on the bridge. Over the rail the mill glowed in the eerie dawn fog like something that had risen smoking from the depths and now sat seething and wracked there among the ruins, waiting for them, lit up like a city, the steam boiling from its stacks whitehot against the pale gray sky as if the whole of it was about to shudder and abandon the earth and fill the sky and drag with it the landscape like cloth caught in talons.

"I'm freezin to death," Mace said.

From *Sharpshooter*

Fragments Found on the Field

David Madden

Started February 1, 1893
Still on Holston Mountain

These sketches and memoirs that I have been writing over the past twenty years are inert fragments lying around the cabin, waiting to be assembled. Having read them over, I now want these fragments to go together in some way. I am 45 and have a sense that it is all ending now. Many men are long dead. Later, I will work on them, make them go together.

(1927, 34 years later: I never did this. What I know now, feel, think imagine--I would like to write a book now. But it's too late. I once started to write A BOY'S HISTORY OF THE CIVIL WAR by a Boy Sharpshooter, anonymous, but gave it up).

Long, long ago, an editor down at the Elizabethton newspaper said, "Mr. Carr, why don't you write that book I keep hearing about?"

I said I would, one of these days.

He said, "You're already 50."

I said, no, 40.

"What keeps you from it?"

I said, "It has to be put together just the way they want it, like all the others, and I can't get interested in that."

"Like what?"

"Like putting in the love element, as they call it. I never had any. I mean *book* romance. Somebody once said that the women of Carter County are ugly beyond human conception. Maybe so. I don't compare. I'm not in a position to, looking myself like a cross between Parson Brownlow and Edwin Booth--when I was young. I'm grateful for the ones that do take up with me around here. Always have been ones that will. But that ain't a love element," I told him.

* * *

Folks back in those days, on august occasions, were very fond of the phrase "The Right Man at the Right Time in the Right Place"--they said that of Jefferson Davis and later of Lincoln. Brownlow even said that of Military Governor Andrew Johnson when the parson arrived in Nashville, and when he became Governor himself, folks said Brownlow was "the Wrong Man in the Wrong Place at the Wrong Time." Scaled down to myself, a commoner, how might that phrase, and on what occasions, apply?

* * *

If you understood the words you live and mayhap die by, doesn't that make your experience different from that of folks who know the words a different way? "Sharpshooter," for instance. "Civil War." Others.

* * *

As I align my right eye, my sights, with General Sanders' heart, I cast light upon him, for is not the light of the body the eye? I fire. But my eye is creative. Thus, I think in images. And as I write, "Words become one with things," so sayeth Emerson. Having made words one with things, I think in images, more lucidly.

* * *

In the beginning were the words. Out of the words, The War. The battles are over and lost, but the words, though spoken, are also printed, and remain.

* * *

So much has been said and written about The War, I am stuck dumb. "What you have received as an inheritance from your fathers," we learn from Goethe, "you must possess again in order to make it your own."

* * *

As I read a veteran's memoir, I hear his voice distinctly. "Speak," I say to the book. "I'm listening." What I want, sometimes expect, but less and less often hope to hear, is a voice that will not just tell me what happened, for now I know it is all a blend of facts and illusions, willful and involuntary falsehoods, but some unexpected way of looking at that time--a voice shedding its light.

* * *

I own no books, except *Pilgrim's Progress*, *The Works of Milton*, *The Works of Shakespeare*, *Robinson Crusoe*, *Parson Brownlow's Book*, and *The Bible*. For other books, I am a patron of public libraries, hither and yon. I borrow from the Lawson McGhee Library in Knoxville that Judge Oliver Temple and the Reverend Thomas Humes--both historians--in concert with others set up in 1886. It's a long trip, so sometimes I have to pay fines for tardy returns. And some few I borrow from Washington College at Limestone and a few from the obliging powers down about Elizabethton--the Carters, the Taylors, and the Stovers.

* * *

I have read now all those books about Tennessee that Ramsey read, by Timberlake, Adair, Judge Haywood, Putnam, Breazeale, and John Carr. (I *am*, or was, or will be each of those men.) And I have read Doctor Ramsey's book, and now *I* am making a book. Another god damned book. To recapture, to redeem. (But never to vindicate.)

I keep going back to Adair's *History of the American Indians, of 1775*. It's not so much for his history of the American Indians--from which all tribes are missing except those of the Southeast which he actually knew--but for the 200 pages (half the book) in which he advances 23 arguments for the Indian tribes having descended from the Hebrew tribes that I read him. All this I read again and again, as romance. But I see with some force that in following another man's romantic obsession as he argues for its actuality, the facts he enlists come clearer than if I had gotten them straight, undiluted by romantic vision, and that I am simultaneously transported as no blatant romance in itself has ever done.

* * *

Where do *my* fragments fit in? A contribution or a distraction?

* * *

The historian plunges into the Unknown, sometimes the bizarre, because what is unknown and bizarre attracts him, but then all his effort are to domesticate it. Too many historians have the minds of public accountants. Knowing the end of each episode, the historian, no less than the fictioneer, pretends, thus distorts, while claiming objectivity. History, as I read it on the mountain, is replete with splendid irrelevancies, and unactualized possibilities.

It is strange--how can it ever be familiar--to stand in a library on your own two feet and face one hundred and twenty eight volumes of *The War of the Rebellion Official Records* and realize that all of it is *there*, there it all is, what the war generated, day by day, but no one man had it all at his command, not even Lincoln, certainly not the generals, most of them dead before the first five volumes appeared in 1880, even more absolutely not the soldier in the ranks, few of whom live today to gaze upon the row on row of thick tomes. More volumes came out in 1890-1891 and the rest will come out in 1901, complete. The official facts--even so, too many wrong, distorted, unverifiable, some adrift, like smoke thinning over a battlefield.

But there we had it at last, and the impact of those 128 volumes was to shatter many memoirs as basic authorities for historians. The editors had omnipotence when they commenced to hand us the day's mail, for each day, enabling us to hear the voices of the officers and statesmen (Reverend William Blount Carter's, Doctor Ramsey's, Parson Brownlow's, General Sanders'--though not Cherokee's, not mine) as God heard them, to see The War day by day as God saw it. But they willed to give it all to us in pigeon-holes, departments, compartments, according to campaigns, battles, et cetera, and then the historians come along and put all that stuff in their own departments and compartments.

When I can get my hands on them, I roam through them, and I want to read each of those 128 volumes, I am indeed mesmerized, but I always leave them with a feeling of profound dissatisfaction that soon turns to melancholy. They are a melancholy necessity.

* * *

Brownlow's newspapers, books, diary, letters, and Ramsey's history, autobiography, and letters, among with my own scraps, fragments, and sketches, are talking leaves, making rustling sounds that conjure echoes and images of Sequoyah, the silversmith-wordsmith, lost in Mexico, and Cherokee, reading his Phoenix newspaper in the sun on the dead-line at Andersonville.

* * *

I tried to meet Parson Brownlow (the prison encounter doesn't count). I tried to meet Doctor Ramsey.

Then I got to where I did not want to anymore. Fear, I reckon. Then it was too late. One morning in 1877, Parson Brownlow supervised repair on his back porch on East Cumberland and lay down to rest and never got up. He died April 29, at the age of 72. Seven years later, in 1884, Doctor Ramsey, at New Mecklenburg, a few blocks above Brownlow on East Main Street, died on April 11, at the age of 87, from "advanced age, together with injuries he received by being thrown from a horse some ten years ago." "Too late" is a phrase I hear more and more often.

Doctor Ramsey is buried where he planned to be, and ought to be, among his family, in the cemetery of the church of Lebanon in the Forks, and Brownlow is buried ambiguously in Old Gray Cemetery, where lies Ramsey's son Crozier, arch enemy of Brownlow, and perhaps a few other Confederate soldiers.

* * *

Came in a dream last night, this phrase, which I will simply set down: "Whereas whistling is darkness made visible, death is...."

* * *

That interests me, how people you never meet affect you, as much as, perhaps more than, the soldiers you clashed with on the Sunken Road, in The Bloody Angle, in The Hornet's Nest, on the ice-slick slopes of Fort Sanders. Davis and Lincoln obviously. Generals Lee and Grant, obviously. General Longstreet and General Sanders. But what about all the others? They all determine who you were. But only if one day you come to know it, before it really is too late. Doesn't it amaze you that General Lee, who knew Generals Stonewall Jackson, Jeb Stuart, and Old Pete Longstreet, and "Little Powell" Hill, would answer the question, "Who was the greatest soldier in the Southern Army?" by saying, "A man I have never seen. His name is Forrest."

I can see clearly in my thinking, if not my life, the hand of Brownlow the journalist, of Doctor Ramsey the Historian, of Sequoyah the language-maker, of Brownlow the Orator.

Something in me leaned toward Brownlow and his newspaper shop, and then when I began to hear about Doctor Ramsey, something in me leaned toward Mecklenburg, Lebanon in the Forks. The Carter County bridge burners led me to Brownlow, the Fighting Parson. I discovered Ramsey gradually, as I went along, and as I began to piece my own life together, I inclined toward "the vain old historian," Ramsey before 1845, of that Golden Age, 1815-45, before the Mexican War. But his other roles stirred my imagination too: farmer, banker, railroad man, doctor, wandering treasurer of the Confederacy. Parson Brownlow and Doctor Ramsey walked toward me on Gay Street as grandfathers, and as I grew older, they became fathers, and then they died--"when the father dies the son becomes mortal"--and so they, both now long dead, will one day in the future be my brothers.

* * *

I am, like Orlando Poe and Jedediah Hotchkiss, a Map-Maker, like Bernard and Gardner and O'Sullivan, a photographer, like Alfred Waud and Winslow Homer, an artist. All Yankees.

* * *

That it was a young man's war seems to interest people, though we who were very young then understood so little of how the old folks got us into it. People like to point at the youngest soldier wounded or killed, and you can see them pictured in Miller's *The Photographic History of the Civil War* and hear them set to verse or song here and there.

* * *

The Old Men sow seeds that the young men reap in war. (1927: I have seen it since, in 1898, the Spanish-American War, and in 1914, the Great World War.)

* * *

Doctor Ramsey and Parson Brownlow moved up and down Gay Street like two planets. Knoxville was the hub of Brownlow's newspaper and Ramsey's banking ventures. Ramsey and Brownlow exemplify polar opposite traits in the divided character of East Tennesseans. Someday, I will show you exactly what I mean.

* * *

This image haunts Ramsey: his great-grandmother on his father's side was washed overboard and lost when she and her husband sailed for America from Scotland. No image haunts Brownlow.

* * *

I have meditated on words; on writings about the war, on books in general, on my own writings as re-read and as in progress. Reckon they will let me read out all I have written here to them between the speeches of the Generals? I missed the Fort Sanders reunion of 1890 at Knoxville and the one at Bethel Cemetery in Knoxville this year. But somewhere, there will be another one, soon.

* * *

As I read the Civil War memoirs, I look for a passage, a line, a footnote that sparks me as I was, or *maybe* was, or may have been. Survivors, marching without direction back and forth over these fields of print. These books are reunions and memorials.

* * *

North and South, like Brownlow and Ramsey, cite the same passages from the Bible, as if God were glib. Walking the mountain at twilight, they might hear God's voice, very faintly, "I am not what you think I am."

* * *

In their use of God's Word, this War between brothers was a gang rape of God.

* * *

In my own vision, Brownlow the fire-eater started out as Lucifer, while Ramsey the old Southern Gentleman, started out as Christ. Came a time when I began to see how their qualities were mixed.

* * *

Ramsey and Brownlow each in his own way strove to put death in its Place. Ramsey felt certain he lived in a place. Brownlow lived only in his description of a place. (Home, Knoxville, the Union.) He *was* the descriptions he cast out to the public. He existed in what *seemed*. He fabricated the world. Ramsey looked upon the world a thing already made, by God. The War stripped away the placeness of Ramsey's life, but Brownlow, whose place was the creation of his own seemings and his own descriptions, was unchanged; peace and war to Brownlow were of the same process, with only word distinctions.

* * *

For Ramsey, Christ was alive in every moment, in all life's forms, rituals, offices, relations, family, etc. He is continuously there. For Brownlow, Christ was alive only when spoken of--he is newly risen from the dead in the Word spoken. The Word proves he has risen.

Ramsey sees manifestations of God, and in the work of his own hand feels the presence of God. Brownlow feels God only in his own mouth and in his own ear, magnified by other ears hearing him, or by hearing other mouths like his own.

Place, and life in it, ceases to be mundane for Brownlow during moments of fiery speech. For Ramsey, place, and life in it, is always momentous.

For Ramsey, the body of Christ and of history is *there* and language describes it, but for Brownlow until words are spoken, turning words into body, there is no body. That is why meditation on the made-world is Ramsey's mode, while constant speaking is Brownlow's.

Brownlow thinks he can talk his way out of being an animal. Ramsey's meditation tells him that he has never been an animal.

Both men fail repeatedly, but try again, condemned to create.

* * *

The god-like Generals were often petty. But so were the Greek Gods. Wasn't that part of their appeal? That they raised "life" to a higher plane? A petty God is higher than a petty mortal.

* * *

Good is the ambience of all human action. Evil exists only *in* isolated acts of good.

* * *

God is simultaneously the infinite extension of the finite, the finite inversion of the infinite. God is the infinite finite. Everywhere I walk on this mountain, I see evidence of this.

* * *

Cherokee, sometimes I wish you had never taught me to read and write, so that I would be forced to draw pictures.

I could capture it all best, image and emotion and idea, in Chinese ideograms, but you can't read them, and I can't draw them. Still, it's the primacy of the image.

* * *

Parson Brownlow was like John Randolph, in a backwoods way, totally individualist, Davy Crockett, a braggart always ready to go, Mike Fink, folk hero, Sut Lovingood, the wise rube, Lincoln, the folksy President, Andrew Johnson, the combative President, St. John, "the Word made flesh."

Doctor Ramsey was like General Lee, the gentleman bound to duty, Calhoun, the defender of states' rights, St. Paul, the thought is the same as the deed, Job, the sufferer of great calamities, modified by the Presbyterian injunction not to murmur.

* * *

I see in Brownlow's life a demonstration of the destiny of Western Man, who is condemned to respond to objects. I feel the pathos of strictly utilitarian objects that are still useful but remain unused: A bridge. A church. A graveyard. A furnace. A hammer. A flute. Brownlow at 72. A locomotive. A photo negative. A telescopic lens, detached.

* * *

In half sleep came the phrase "a Separational Unity." Does that phrase describe the relation of North and South from the start?

* * *

What does that mean--the shoe is on the other foot? Is anything ever really alien? I read somewhere that every lefthanded person lost a twin in the womb, and that the twin was absorbed into the mother, leaving an empty sack. Ramsey and Brownlow--did one of them *almost* stay enwombed?

* * *

I have made a list of the histories of the War that I intend to find and read, and beside the ones that sound the best, I have made a cross mark.

+ *Battles and Leaders,* 1887
+ *Is Davis a Traitor?* by Alfred I. Bledsoe, 1866

The Rise and Fall of the Confederate Government by Jefferson Davis, 1881
Some biographies:
+ *The Prison Life of Jefferson Davis* by John J. Craven, 1866.
Life and Campaigns of Lt. Gen. Thomas J. Jackson by R. L. Dabney, 1866
The Life and Campaigns of J.E.B. Stuart by H. B. McClellan, 1885
A fusilage of Generals and Privates now get into the act:
John B. Hood, *Advance and Retreat*, 1880
+ Basil Duke, *History of Morgan's Calvary*, 1866
Joseph E. Johnston, *Narrative of Military Operations*, 1874
+ J. B. Jones, *A Rebel War Clerk's Diary*, 1866
+ Sam R. Watkins, *Co. "Atych," A Side Show of the Big Show*
+ Phoebe Pember, *A Southern Woman's Story*, 1879
+ Belle Boyd, *In Camp and Prison*,
Wearing of the Gray by John Esten Cooke, 1867
Christ in the Camp by J. William Jones, 1888
History of the Confederate States Navy by J. Thomas Scharf, 1887 (I missed that part totally)

* * *

Can you simultaneously think of a chair as molecules--though that was not possible before 1811--*and* sit on it? History is land-locked water in which I am a sponge. History is the dialectic of the living and the dead. Count the votes of the dead at unwatched polling places. Do I have, among all these fragments the years have left behind, a synthesis?

* * *

The historical self is mere chance. In the recreation of others, I become myself. The personal rots. I am what survives me. To act is to witness, to witness is to act. Then, the emphasis was on the act. Now, the emphasis is on witnessing. Then and now, I act and witness simultaneously.

* * *

I sometimes see the image of the naked body, male not female, why is that? and think of the phrase "the body politic."
This I know: God is in nature and man is made in nature's image. Man is shaped like a five pointed star: a head, two arms, two legs. The head itself is a star composed of five parts, too: skull, eyes, ears, nose, mouth. Each hand, each foot has five points. Each hand may reach for the stars, even as each foot treads the ground. Star-shaped man simultaneously is also cross-shaped. Man has two of everything: eyes,

ears, nostrils, mouth and bung-hole are further apart, two arms, hands, legs, feet, except, only one head, one private. All the elements of nature are alive in man: air, water, earth, fire enter through the mouth, exit through the bung and the dong. Sounds enter, fumes enter, and through the eyes, the windows of the soul, light enters. The anus mimics hell, the heart is emblematic of heaven, the guts are the labyrinth of Crete, and the genitals recreate man even as they excrete man's waste. The right hand is fact, pulls the trigger. The lefthand is imagination. We have two opposable thumbs, each of which is a machine, which together make up a super machine. Writing, it seems odd that one thumb must lie useless as the other converts a piece of wood-encased lead into a machine that records the body's own description.

Is slavery an inflammation of the body politic? Cherokee.

* * *

When the Confederates occupied Knoxville, Ramsey was influential; when the Union occupied it, he was exiled. The Confederates jailed and exiled Brownlow; the Union made him a powerful administrator. I see parallel images of their wandering. At different periods, each was on the run: Ramsey on back roads in the mountains and in many cities carrying the bank of Tennessee and of the Confederacy, on trains, horses, on foot, in wagons. Brownlow is a fugitive in the mountains, then he tours the cities of the North as exile, also gathering (but not, like Ramsey, dispersing) money or the cause, his own cause, his newspaper, so that he can serve the larger cause, the Union, which is another way of serving his personal cause.

* * *

Warm-hearted among family and friends, Brownlow made many enemies and engaged in a few street fights and was once ambushed at night. A club wound on his head affected his behavior thereafter. He was fearless and reckless. He once wrote to a friend about attending a religious conference. "Should they not kill me, I will leave for the Convention Thursday next." A friend once asked his advice in dealing with a foe: "Lather him with nitric acid and shave him with a hand saw."

* * *

Ramsey never becomes violent, although his soldier sons, especially Robert, do; Brownlow, physically, is seldom violent but his violent utterances and publications incite all kinds of violence. Ramsey does incite violence against Brownlow, and Brownlow against him. They seldom mention each other in public, although Brownlow attacks

Ramsey's sons and other relatives; and Ramsey's sons and relatives attack him. Brownlow always carried a pistol and kept one in his desk at the newspaper but never shot a man. He always tried to kill the soul of his enemies with fear; psychological terror made of Tennesseans for four years nervous wrecks. He preached vengeance instead of orderly development. Violence as a community effort becomes an extra-community in itself.

* * *

Brownlow boasts that he never drank, chewed, smoked, attended theatres or race tracks, that he courted only one woman and "her I married." He was always ready to step forward as a character reference for himself. Brownlow was accused of many crimes but never of personal dishonesty, drunkenness, or licentiousness. "He could express more vituperation and scorching hate than any half a dozen men that ever appeared in American politics," a historian said of him. "The man was a strange compound, and there are no more like him." "In politics, religion, journalism his work and his fame were temporary. He was a product of his times, but his times produced no one like him. His style of journalism passed before he did." He wronged many individuals, "dropped the bitterness of gall into many a cup of happiness," caused many a wreck of hopes and ambition. But some say he had high moral and intellectual qualities, though no sense of fitness or taste. Ramsey had innate good taste. If, as some say, a man's character is revealed in his choice of jokes (and his sense of humor), what am I to say of Ramsey, who had one, and of Brownlow, who had none? The comic figure is unshockable.

* * *

As polar parts of the body politic, Ramsey inhales life, but Brownlow exhales--an action like birth, like cannon.

* * *

Ramsey is a meditative person whose actions are clearly directed and succinctly executed--a man of action in the most civilized sense. Brownlow is an imaginative person who hardly acts at all--his utterances are his acts, like rocks breaking windows. Brownlow is sometimes like a ventriloquist's dummy for which he is his own ventriloquist. When he ruins his voice from too much loud speechifying, someone has to read his speeches while he sits or stands on the platform. In a sense, his newspapers and his books are dummies, through which he speaks, in a style that is more oral than literary. This compulsion of mine to picture things, I share with Brownlow, to reason,

I share with Ramsey. Brownlow had a naive wisdom that I sometimes share.

* * *

Today I am 46. I have just re-read all these fragments. I have decided to quit making these stabs at the bull's eye. No more. It is over with.

* * *

I have made a list of Novels and Romances about the War that I plan to read.

+ = The ones that sound the best.

Micaria, or Altars of Sacrifice, by Augusta Evans, 1864.

+ *Cudjo's Cave* by John Townsend Trowbridge, 1864

+ *Surrey of Eagle's Nest, or, The Memoirs of a Staff Officer Serving in Virginia*, by John Esten Cooke, 1866

+ *Tiger-lilies* by Sidney Lanier, 1867 (set at Mountvale in the Smokies)

Miss Ravenel's Conversion From Secession to Loyalty by John William de Forrest, 1867

+ *A Fool's Errand by One of the Fools* by Albion Winegar Trougee, 1879

His Sombre Rivals by E.P. Roe, 1883

+ *Where the Battle Was Fought* by Charles Egbert Craddock (really Mary Noailles Murfree of Murfreesboro, a lame spinster), 1884

Dr. Sevier, George Washington Cable, 1885

The Red Badge of Courage by Stephen Crane, 1885

+ *The Story of Don Miff, As told by His Friend John Bouche Whacker: A Symphony of Life* by Virginius Dabney, 1886

+ *Tales of Soldiers and Civilians* by Ambrose Bierce, 1891

On the Plantation: A Story of A Georgia Boy's Adventures During the War by Joel Chandler Harris, 1892.

* * *

It is the union of memory and reason, controlling emotion, that unites the past and the present, and no book I have read has done that. Facts help to discipline not only the intellect but emotion and imagination, too. It is the public's impassioned memory that transforms facts into myth. We have not developed an image of our public experience in The War because scholars fear the emotions and the imagination, and fiction writers fear the intellect, and each man knows not how to balance emotion and intellect to discipline the imagination. Memoirs and novels are part of the popular ceremonies that unify us as a nation. All this is theory-thinking and theory is cold. But why is my brain-pan smoking?

* * *

Oh, yes, the war was THE ILIAD and THE ODYSSEY and THE AENEID, Homer and Virgil, all over again. Many say so. Often. What the Greeks set in motion can never be still. The patterns, the parallels are all laid out, unalterable, irreversible, predictable. Cassandra was not silent this time either. This time, the slave girl Helen wore deadly blackface. How do you recapture lost times, if you just keep seeing these god damned parallels to THE BIBLE, Old and New Testament, to Homer, to Virgil, to Milton, to plots laid down in old books? And it's only half-finished, over. Like Dickens--to be continued. A man must resist the strong temptation to drift into allegory. Because allegory does not thrive on multiple interpretations. Satire seems inappropriate. The War will not be mocked.

* * *

Books get hell from everybody, readers and writers right along with illiterates. Schools and books lose out to the college of hard knocks. But by now most of The War is only in books, eyewitnesses, and imaginary accounts, and in the memories of survivors, most of whom are in their 50's. But most memories are inaccessible, even now. And what happens when us veterans are all dead? Then it's all romances-- the repetition of stories veterans told, and of books before and to come. If fragments of facts and romantic vapors are all that are left, the war is missing, or seen in fits and starts, epileptically.

I'm the last of the Willises, so when I go down, these fragments are all that's left--and maybe glimpses of me in books by other men I know not of.

* * *

I set down here words that came in a dream: "The first to declare no clear air marked your word."

* * *

For Ramsey, first the deed, then the Word. He writes the fragments of his autobiography five years after the events of the war. One senses his classical training. His narrative is full of incident but immersed in meditation. Brownlow's words, spoken in debate or written, are his deeds--thus he writes his first autobiography when he is 37, and writes two more during the war, in all three instances attached to polemics on religious or political issues and always made up of fragments of previous writings. I see the influence of backwoods evangelical rhetoric combined with flowery Elizabethan and Miltonic style, and the influence of stump politics and yellow journalism. His narratives lack incident except to illustrate issues, and is immersed in epithets. Ramsey writes in the tradition of Homer and the Bible--to pay homage to ancestors and provide continuity for those who come after him.

* * *

The Civil War action was a kind of violent rhetoric, but after The War, it was rhetoric that made it real to both participants and nonparticipants. Since the masters Aristotle and Cicero formulated the methods, four notions of rhetoric have evolved. The public concept is that the purpose of rhetoric, as in Brownlow's use of it, is to obscure reality. That, of course, is bad rhetoric. Ramsey would say that good rhetoric reveals or reflects reality.

Rhetoric is an essential art for it can change minds and thus change reality through the techniques of persuasion, mutual inquiry (forensic); it can change our sense of past, present, and future. We must distinguish among the kinds of things rhetoric makes. The future is made in how we talk about it now. Rhetoric can be like bullets, determining who lives, who dies. There is practical, pragmatic discourse to deal with realities.

* * *

Ramsey is a private person duty-bound to public service, a contributor to the historical process. Brownlow is a totally public person, from whom all issues flow. Brownlow made historical events, religious and political, so personal, he was, in a sense, outside history.

* * *

The head and shoulders of Doctor Ramsey, painted in 1877, the year Parson Brownlow died, by Lloyd Branson, hung in Mecklenburg Place on Main Street. The larger than life full-length portrait of Governor Brownlow, artist unknown, painted in 1866 at the expense of $1,000 to the taxpayers, hangs still in the State Capitol Building at Nashville. Lawmakers still spit tobacco juice on it, and people of the area, including some of the old mountain unionists who turned on him when he ran over them, spit on it.

. * * *

I heard a boy in Carter County ask his pap, "Who won the War?" His pap said, "Son, it don't really make much difference who won the whole war. In East Tennessee, everybody lost!"

* * *

And I am not the only American who lost the war, and is still looking for it.

* * *

People seem to love to reach for odd facts about the war. That the accuracy of both Rebels and Yankees, for instance, was so poor it took about a man's body weight in lead to kill each soldier. Now here's something not many people remember: The last shot of the War was fired by a Confederate steamer at a Yankee whaler in the Bering Straits where you enter the Arctic Ocean--three months after surrender at Appomattox--a blank. Do you remember that? Did you ever know it? I didn't.

And they love to ponder all kinds of "What if....?" questions about the war. "What if General Longstreet had taken Doctor Ramsey's advice as to the actual position on the French Broad's confluence with the Holston River?" That "What if" is obliterated when you ask, "What if Sherman had allowed Thomas to invade East Tennessee, as planned, after the burning of the bridges in the Great Valley?" Why are they so eager to get the facts, individually and sectionally and nationally? So it will end at last? Then why for me has it yet to begin?

* * *

In a copy of PARSON BROWNLOW'S BOOK, I found the former owner's marginal comment: "When I heard Parson Brownlow tell all this in his orations at Cincinnati, I took all this as Gospel Truth, but I know now much of it is lies and the rest is gross distortion." He does not go on to state, because he probably does not perceive, that the orations, given backbone by the book after, made everything so real that the so-called facts were part of nobody's experience. What is this man's afterthought compared with the burning moment of "Gospel Truth"? To deny or reject the facts of imagination is the dim-wittest kind of romancing of facts.

* * *

The romantic ivy pulls down the house in time. Is that how it should be?

* * *

The phrase "common sense" is a contradiction. Reality is over-rated, passe. Most of the pleasures of this world are imaginary. The rest are merely actual. Not the bear I find, but the bear I hunt. I am not what I eat, I am what I *imagine*. Is there then no reality, only various and workable fictions?

Memory is imagination. What I felt then will never return. But what I feel about what I imagine.... The mysterious ways the imagination works. As if a man writes a letter to a man across the world, not knowing that the man is already dead, and then the writer dies before the letter reaches the address of the dead man, but somehow the letter comes into *my* hands and I read it and it changes my life. Thinking sets off an explosion of possibilities, the fragments fall where they may. Emotions root me, imagination and intellect transport me. I still stand in awe and wonderment before it all.

* * *

As events occurred, something kept me from experiencing them. Now that those events are memories, they are much more accessible, affect me much more piercingly like a pin-prick or a toothache or striking my crazybone.

Sometimes, things I remember that I actually did or saw I mistakenly think I only imagined while in the Tower.

* * *

I forgot to put this one in *The Annals*, thinks Doctor Ramsey. Mr. Audubon tells of the time Daniel Boone told him of an instance of his remarkable memory. He had been captured in the Green River Area of Kentucky by Indians, who got drunk on his own whiskey, so that he was able to slip away, but first he hacked three knotches in an ash tree to mark the spot.

Twenty years later, a friend told him he was having trouble establishing the boundary of some land he was claiming in court but that some men who lived nearby had told him that Boone had marked an ash tree right on the boundary years ago, so he asked Boone to come and go with him to the spot. The landscape had changed greatly, and Boone was sad to see the disappearance of deer and buffalo in that area. But he felt as if he were still captive of the Indians, his memory was so lucid. The tree showed no signs of knotches, but Boone took an ax from one of the men who had accompanied him and his friend and began to scrape away at the bark. Slowly, the three distinct knotches were revealed. I think I would not forget where I buried the depositary of the Confederacy, even twenty years from now, thinks Doctor Ramsey.

* * *

Lost Cause? Since the war, mostly Virginia has kept that up, focusing on Lee. But there never was a Cause for me, or for other East Tennesseans, certainly not for the Mountain North Carolinians, who died 4 to 1 compared with any other state (six times more than

Tennessee). We fought to maintain the honor and wealth of the Old Virginia Dominion that had already faded into the past and for the new Cotton South's money.

* * *

One fact too many and the imagination balks, one feels atrophy in the brain. The problem is not so much an inability to experience the holocaust as a failure in the aftermath to imagine it.

* * *

While the battle of Gettysburg--the high tide of the Confederacy--was going on, two tribes in Africa were slaughtering each other--the map screams of it. They, too, must have an historian. But how can I make of their event something significant, as Marx, a Russian writer, was readily able to make of the American Civil War in his articles for The New York *Daily Tribune* and a Vienna newspaper.

And in the Makan desert of China nothing was happening.

* * *

I'm not trying to be elusive--allusive, yes. So much eludes me that....

* * *

Perhaps we should, in fact, *say* those things that, we say, *go_without* saying.

* * *

Parson Brownlow missed the bridge burning, as I did.

Both Brownlow and Doctor Ramsey missed General Sanders' Raid and the Siege of Knoxville.

Both Parson Brownlow and Doctor Ramsey missed the war.

They're both whirling in their graves as Knoxville changes from year to year.

* * *

Missing in action? They'll deal you the statistics. But weren't we all? Even Grant? Read his memoirs, the best of the bunch. Even he is missing in action. Jeff Davis was missing since Buena Vista. Bragg since West Point. Well, I exaggerate.

The sense of having missed myself plagued me all across the plains. When I reached the Rockies, it was like Shelley coming around the corner of his house on the balcony at Lerieci and meeting himself.

Obsessed with this sense of having missed the war, I turned to the man I thought I had killed. But General Sanders was elusive, so I reached for Reverend Carter, and Brownlow, and then for Doctor Ramsey.

Charged image cliches first attracted me to Sanders, to Carter, to Brownlow, and Ramsey. Brownlow's voice, hot in my ear. The sense of Ramsey's omniscience as an historian. The man-of-action image of Reverend Carter, firing the bridges.

I knew I had fought in it, but as I learned that I knew nothing about it, animal curiosity took hold of me. The discovery that I might have killed General Sanders.... And through him, I became curious about Carter, Brownlow, and Ramsey. From general curiosity, I moved into guilt, a motive for repossessing the events, the specific events of his death, to general events. And then, compulsion, to experience it all: see it: beyond curiosity, guilt, nostalgia. I passed through moods of cynicism, even pessimism, and then of Rabelaisian mockery, like Sut Lovingood. But over all--this compulsion to repossess those years.

* * *

I want to look at it every way there is to look at it. Look at it this way: General Sanders' circulatory system could encircle the world four times--and, mine, of course, and yours.

* * *

I think of the many men who sent substitutes and so missed the war.

* * *

Is it any wonder so many missed so much of the war? Somebody, I forget who, asked, "Can you count the spokes, of a turning wheel?" Of whom did he ask that question? Regarding what? And when? And why?

* * *

Forgiveness restores innocence for a moment, and to be innocent is to begin again. Better the certainty of experience than beginning again.

* * *

I'm still not certain. If the hand that shot General Sanders had become like the dyer's hand, red always, I would have known the first time the question was raised, but I would, if mine had not been red, have written none of these fragments, and I would have lived alone on this mountain or alone in some populous city.

* * *

The sense of everyone else dying in *my* death fills me more with compassion for all the others than with fear or pity for myself. I do not want to die, because when I die, I feel, the whole world dies with me. I feel pathos for the death of everyone but myself. That is only *two* ways of saying the same thing.

* * *

Each of these writings is a shell fragment, a nail in one of these cluster bombs.

* * *

If we are not mute, but speak, if we can read and write, are we condemned by words to create?

* * *

Remember. Repent. Return.

* * *

Of course, what is most important remains unwritten.

* * *

Brownlow's KNOXVILLE WHIGS are no more. They caught fire somehow and, being dry and brittle, almost burned down my cabin, but I went tearing out the front door with my arms full of them and tossed them like a flock of burning birds into the air, risking burning the whole mountain, for the slopes are dry and brittle, too, in September.

* * *

Only voices now, only echoes.

* * *

I always intended all these fragments for my family, but I have never had any children. I am by my lonesome.

December 12, 1893

I'm ready, I think, to write about the shooting of General Sanders, but not about the shooting of Cherokee, who taught me how to read.

Outrider

Miles Wilson

They approached the high basin from the south, riding single file, three watersheds north of the Staked Plains. The Marshal rode in front, whistling an air from Schubert. Behind him, reins slack in his bandaged hands, came a second man. A little distance back, and just to the right out of the dust drift, the third rider followed, eyes gritted. They circled down to the basin floor and swung into the October sun, through sage, juniper, and chaparral, all afternoon to the western flank of the bowl.

The cabin hardly seemed an artifact. Sod and stone and aspen logs, it looked as though it had simply risen there. The man had expected adobe. It was his only expectation.

The horses blew and browsed and the wind came up a little. The Marshal waited beside the second man while the deputy remained an edgy distance behind them. Finally, the man with the broken hands got down. The Marshal leaned across and cut free the man's saddlebags and bedroll. The deputy cam up then, taking the hanging reins, and the Marshal set down a Winchester in its scabbard and on top of it a gun belt with a long-barreled Colt in the holster. The deputy rearranged his angle in the saddle.

"Keep in touch." The deputy had been waiting to say it all the way out, and the waiting had given it just the edge he wanted.

Long after they were gone, before he entered the cabin, the man flared his head back and sent a seared, stammering howl into the cavity of air far across the basin.

"I'd never go out like that." In his duster, the deputy popped in the wind. He didn't like to make noise, but the weather had turned on them. Already, pellets of sleet buckshot his back. They would camp two nights in the early snow before they got down and south of it.

"No, J.T., you wouldn't."

"I'd sooner go farm or clerk; I'd sooner be blowed the hell away. No one to go up against. You'd get stale, lose your touch. Even him."

"Out there, he goes against Leit and Corder and Benecelli."

"They're all dead."

55

"Yes."

The sleet was beginning to rime the deputy's moustache. The Marshal, ruddy and clean-shaven, drew a woolen muffler across his face.

"I expect you got your reasons, but I can't see it. You ask me, I'd say plant him and be shut of it. Or bring him in, like Lever." J.T.'s face was raw and livid as welt. "Maybe I just don't see the big picture, how it's all supposed to turn out."

"Perhaps we'll get around to that sometime."

"If we have to?"

"If I have to."

The woman had been there two days before the man understood that he had not made her up. He kept her one day after that, and she stayed two more on her own. He had not seen another person in three years. She asked about his work, and he spoke freely. The last night she came at him with a knife as he slept. He caught the little intake of breath as she raised the knife and rolled off the bunk at her legs, still not quite awake, too slow to just knock her down, coming fully awake at the terrible popping of ligaments in her knee. In the morning, she was an hour saddling up, and once mounted could not hold the stirrup with her bad leg.

"And that's all?" The Marshal was massaging oil into the rosewood desk with his palm. "You're quite sure there is nothing else?"

"Quite. His appetites were unnatural, of course. It was more graphic than any fantasy of J.T.'s and as subtle as your history. But I know how pornography bores you."

She leaned into her cane getting up. The Marshal wondered if he should keep using dancers. They were the best athletes he knew of and had done well enough in the past, but they were sticklers for form, always a little rehearsed and self-aware, always beatable by intuition and reflex.

"And his eyes?"

The woman stopped but did not look back.

"Gray. Gray going to agate. Some graininess in the whites in the sun."

Wilson

When Lever came to see him, the man caught the movement first, far out on the basin floor, and knew it was Lever as soon as he made out his odd gait in the saddle. He and Lever had been close, years ago when they rode together, but they had lost touch except by reputation. Lever rode straight in, and slowly, giving the man plenty of time. He sighted him in the last three hundred yards. Lever came past the stand of aspen whistling, and the man moved out of the trees behind him.

"No need for that," said Lever. He pulled up, unhooked his gun belt, and stepped down, slinging the belt across his saddle. Instinct, the man thought, or had he made some noise? No, instinct. Lever walked up, his head at an odd angle, as though his neck had been broken.

"Just in the neighborhood and thought I'd see how you were making out. If there was anything I could do. You can put that away. Look here." Lever wiggled his fingers at his eyes. A creamy haze. "Ten, maybe fifteen percent at the sides; straight on it's as black as my heart."

They talked mostly about the old days until all the whiskey Lever had brought was gone. Then Lever talked very carefully about the new days.

"I'm seen to," he said. "You should see my reviews. They made it so easy there's nothing to it, even with these." He thumbed his eyes. "Let me show you."

They went outside with the whiskey bottles. Lever strapped on his gun belt and the man stood behind him, the Colt tucked in his pants.

"Just off either shoulder, any height."

Lever picked the neck off the first, pitched in an easy arc, and shattered the second, a spinner. The third came past him waist-high, fifteen feet out and humming. It exploded at his second shot. And he came on around, in a crouch, head swiveling like a turret, and there was no one there. Lever straightened up and fired his last two shots into the dirt.

"I was always quicker, but you was always smarter."

The man moved out of the cabin; he had stepped back with each toss and had thrown the last bottle from the doorway.

"Go on, then." Lever cartwheeled his pistol as high as the aspen and the man took off the trigger and hammer on the way up.

Lever retrieved the pistol. "Well, then, I guess I'll be getting along. Unless there's something else."

Wilson

The man shot off both of Lever's index fingers at the second knuckle.

The Marshal had to spend a long time with Lever before he got most of the truth out of him. He had closed the drapes to spare Lever the glare from the courtyard. He liked the husky light in the room, and left them drawn when the sun passed from the courtyard.

"How the hell am I going to get along with these?" Lever splayed his hands on the desk, smudging the finish. The Marshal sighed. Lever disappointed him.

"With mechanical aids, or a ghostgunner; perhaps a *doppelganger*. You may count on our support as long as you do nothing embarrassing. Understand, however, that the main circuit is now out of the question."

"You bastards. What if I told the truth?"

The rasping swish of clippers sheared the air in the room as the gardener pruned the boxwood back. The Marshal sat still in the dead center of Lever's vision.

"I was just talking; I mean, I'm pretty worked up, that's all."

"Yes. You were going to tell me about his eyes."

"Well, I did the best I could. Pig iron, I'd say."

"And the whites?"

"Clear. Oh, Jesus, I haven't seen any that bright since Sammy Shaniko."

Lever started to cry, a sort of jerky hiccuping that he tried to talk through. At times like these, the Marshal was sure he should have gone into banking.

"He can be got, Marshal, I swear it. It took him four shots to pick my pistol apart. I looked it all over. He missed it clean twice. Let J.T. at him; J.T. could take him out."

When Lever was gone, the Marshal lit the lamps and wiped down his desk. J.T. might indeed be able to do it; he certainly wanted to do it, even after riding ahead of Lever and working his way down the rim with glasses. Of his four shots, the man had fired the first two into the dirt. J.T. was good, but the Marshal couldn't risk it. A man as fast and mean and stupid as J.T. was not a prize to squander. They still turned them out mean and stupid, but fast was a gift. It could not be arranged.

They went back in July, under an operatic sky. The Marshal had hoped for Wagnerian weather, had waited for it six weeks once he made up his mind. The spectral cumulus and prismatic sunsets exceeded his expectations. J.T. was bileful. The Marshal had been firm about his part in it. He had bought one day of silence by seeing to it that J.T. set out with a glacial hang-over; he got two more days of sulk. He could manage two days of talk.

"I'd let him rot. I'm telling you, if it was up to me I'd leave it the hell alone. Not that it's much of a chance after all this time. If he was coming back, he'd come by now. Not a word in years. Why mess with it?"

"Because he didn't quit or change."

"How the hell do you know?"

"I have made it a point to know what I needed to."

"What finally gets to them in the end? Money, pussy, a big name? Just wearing out?"

"Yes. Also, they respect me."

J.T. broke a raw laugh. "They hate your guts."

"That too."

"What about him?"

"I'm not certain yet."

"I thought you knew everything."

"If this didn't take some discretion, any shootist could do it."

"Even me, I suppose."

"I suppose."

The fifth day out, coming into the chalk hills that marked the edge of the basin, they flushed a band of ravens that detonated from a carcass in the brush, spooking the horses. The riderless roan broke away, and they lost six miles running him down. It also cost them the sun, and they made camp early, waiting for morning. The Marshal wanted to go in with the sun low and at his back.

"Have I ever told you, J.T. that you are without peer in healing berserkers?" The Marshal dropped in an extra measure of coffee and chicory for the pot.

"Nobody ever had to. I never seen anybody handle them any better."

"Yes, they are best dealt with among us, and directly. But I must tell you that berserkers hold little interest for me anymore; I am grateful that I can trust them to you. But the others--few enough, *bien entendu*--the ones that cannot be healed, gone into the weather, the outriders, J.T. ..."

The deputy was bored.

"How many you figure you brought back?"

The Marshal settled the pot into the coals. He had been talking to himself again. He would have to see that cellist when they got back.

"As many as I had to."

The Marshal left J.T. on the rim with glasses. He was to come in only after it was over, or if something went wrong. The Marshal led the horses down and was well out on the basin floor by first light. Whenever he was away from the basin, he used it as the measure of earthworks, yet when he was in it he saw how little it left to the imagination. There probably an article for someone in that.

As he approached the stand of aspen, the Marshal saw that the man had stripped bark from the trunks and main limbs. He had been careful not to disturb the inner bark; not all of them had been such attentive botanists. If the aspen were not so prolific, the residents so few, the grove would have been gone by now. The Marshal was certain the man was not in the grove, but he was almost as sure he was not in the cabin. The scrolls of aspen were stretched on a lattice of drying racks to the side of the cabin. The Marshal aimed his horse towards them, stopping forty feet out.

"I've come alone." A mistake. The tinny taste came up in his mouth. "I left J.T. on the rim; there is no one else."

The Marshal leaned forward in the saddle and rubbed at a bulge along his horse's jawline. The gelding gummed at the bit, raising a knot of muscles the Marshal had to unravel each night.

The man emerged then from the drying racks, hands like jewelers' scales, balancing his carbine. He moved laterally until the cabin was at his back. The roan sidestepped prissily, swinging out until the tether to the gelding snapped his head around.

"Things have changed," said the Marshal. "You are needed."

The man gestured and the Marshal dropped his gun belt and rifle; the man motioned again, the carbine moving with the elegance and precision of a baton, and the Marshal unsnapped his cuffs and rolled both sleeves above his elbows. He had an awkward time with his boots, but finally managed to wedge them in the stirrups and work his feet out.

"A completely free hand," said the Marshal. "No interference, no adjustments, on whatever terms you name. You have my absolute word."

Behind an Old Testament beard, the man's mouth gave away nothing, but his eyes came unmuzzled and the Marshal fixed them in his memory. They were entire beyond all reckoning.

And the man slackened the Winchester and poured his chest into a rising pillar of triumph and the Marshal stretched again to rub at the gelding's knot and the horse's head leaned aside into the rubbing and with his other hand under the mane, in the pouch sutured to the roots of the mane, he arranged the ivory derringer and moving the gelding a fraction with his knees shot the man very carefully through the throat.

The Marshal tied the horses in the grove. He could see the dust scrawled out behind J.T. as he came headlong down the flank of the bowl. The Marshal walked back to the body. Already, flies had begun to browse the wound. He squatted down. The eyes were almost gone, but as he watched they fissured deep, then filled with sludge.

The Marshal was finishing his inventory when J.T. arrived. J.T. examined the body and grunted his professional admiration.

"You are still one son of a bitch to be reckoned with." Blood made J.T. careless. The Marshal looked up from the scrolls. He had an unflinching respect for certain profanity; it brought bad luck. His analyst, so helpful in other matters, had been unable to dowse the source of this. J.T. had trouble sometimes with the proscribed phrases.

"I mean, Marshal." J.T. didn't like to back up. "I saw him in San Saba once. I was just a kid, but I knew what to look for. He couldn't have got any quicker since. I could have taken him head on."

The Marshal thought about the eyes.

"No."

"What happens now?"

J.T. had gotten the man up on the roan with some trouble, and though the man sat on the horse awkwardly, he would limber up on the ride back. By the time they reached town he would be perfectly at ease, indistinguishable.

"We will absorb him, and sanctify him."

The Marshal's hand was stiff from taking notes. Perhaps J.T. could lean photography. The Marshal heaped all the bark from the cabin around the drying racks. He folded away a sonnet-sized piece and set the pile afire.

"Sanctify?"

"J.T., you had better learn language before your reflexes go. It means to make holy."

"I'd say you made a fair start with that derringer. I still don't see what's so special about him now."

"He will acquire a reputation. And we are safe."

"From him?"

"From ourselves, which have always been plain to him."

"Well why the hell didn't we just get it over with back then? We got better things to do than run around the country like missionaries. It ain't efficient."

"He had to be verified for those who notice such things. That could not have happened among us. He has been etched; now we will ink him with fame. He becomes a reproduction, a recitation."

"Hadn't we ought to shave him? So folks will know who he is?"

J.T. didn't like it. The berserkers were rabid, but that was different. This one looked like a dreaming loony, a Hutterite. The kind you went after with dogs and a picnic lunch. J.T. was scrupulous about several things. He never backshot a man unless he had to, and he left the feebleheaded to the preachers' bountymen.

"It is the mark of wilderness on him, the authentic sign that he is not ours."

"Is he? He ain't much, for sure, but the son of a bitch, I mean, he is still strange. How do you know?"

"I have a strict obligation never to mistake such men. Call it a touch, my gift. A tint, a gesture, an inflection--they assemble themselves into certainty." The Marshal stopped, savored. He felt the shiver of pleasure, almost sexual, at rubbing words together until they

Wilson

came. He also knew that it angered and frightened J.T. He relaxed his grip.

"The way, say, you know a man is going to draw before he knows it himself; who, among strangers, you must always keep in sight on a street; when the tree line conceals an ambush and the moment to break for cover."

"That's just good sense."

"Yes, and you are well rewarded for it."

"I'm alive."

"I suppose."

"Well, it's more than this asshole." He drew and spun off four slugs, then a fifth, exploding the pulpy spine of a yucca. "You think he's something better than me. Like you'd like to throw in with him."

"That is why I am proficient."

They came into town mid-afternoon, the sky almond at their backs, a big blow on the way behind them from the Staked Plains. The Marshal's clerk met them at the ford. There was money at the bank in the man's name; two women lay coiled in bed in his suite at the hotel. The citizens mostly went about their business, but a few spoke and the Marshal returned their greetings by name. As they passed the hotel on their way to the livery, the Marshal was gratified at the number of brokers from the academies, ateliers, and foundations. The porch rail was festooned with their prospectuses. A scout from the Prize and Bounty Consortium lounged in disguise at the hotel bar. At an upper window, an envoy from the Chancellery slanted a specimen bottle into the light.

And the man drew himself up, hesitant until the gesture came, then graceful, nodding left and right like a king.

Thursday

Joanna Leake

The refrigerator broke on Thursday. Mrs. Hammond gave it a single look, daring it to be out of whack, and then went to call the repair service. Mrs. Hammond looked like a bulldog. She had fierce little eyes, a square jaw and short, strong arms that looked as though she had lifted weights or done heavy work. But for all her solid bulldog scrappiness, Mrs. Hammond had a high clear voice that gave a note of sweetness to everything she said. Even if it was to call the refrigerator repair service and ask that somebody please come out today, before all the meat in her freezer just stank to high heaven.

Joe Dinatorri was the refrigerator repairman. He could fix all mechanical appliances. He could fix car engines. He could fix toys and jammed staplers and clogged drains. He could touch a hurt dog that was snarling and snapping and it would lie quiet and just whimper. He went to work six days a week at 6:30 a.m. He went to Mass every Sunday.

"Well, I'm glad to see you," Mrs. Hammond said to Joe Dinatorri. "Come right on in and have a look-see. You two stay out of the man's way," she said to Lucy and Rollo who were playing a game of Battle on the kitchen floor. "Pile your cards up neat and get them out of the way."

Mr. Hammond, the children's father, did not approve of his children playing cards, and he didn't approve of Lucy being called Lucy. He had wanted to name the children something dignified, he said. Lucille and Roland. But never to Mrs. Hammond's recollection had anyone except for Mr. Hammond ever called them anything except Lucy and Rollo. Mr. Hammond had taken sixteen weeks of night school classes and a loss in pay to change from a blue collar to a white collar one at the sweet potato cannery. Mrs. Hammond had to give up her plans to buy a ping pong table. She also had to buy him four drip-dry white shirts and three ties.

"You got a leak in your freezer coil here," said Joe Dinatorri.

"Oh rats. Sounds grim," said Mrs. Hammond. "Will it take you long to fix it?"

"May take a while, but don't you worry."

Mrs. Hammond began washing dishes. Joe Dinatorri began taking the refrigerator apart.

"Hot, ain't it?" said Joe Dinatorri.

"Hot as hades," said Mrs. Hammond. "I suppose that meat in my freezer will be thawed out and stinky before you get the cold air going again."

"I'm afraid so. I'll try and hurry it along but it looks like an all day job to me."

"In this heat it'll spoil by noon."

"Maybe you could take the meat over to a neighbor's until I get you fixed up here."

Mrs. Hammond went over to the freezer and reached over Joe Dinatorri's head to take stock of the meat in her freezing compartment which was going to spoil before her very eyes. Mr. Hammond did not approve of waste. He did not approve of her buying the Family-Sav-R 10-pack of pork chops on special because he did not want the check out girl at the Piggly Wiggly to think that they were scrimping and saving on groceries.

Mrs. Hammond thought a minute. She supposed she could take the pork chops next door and put them in Dolores' freezer. But the truth was that Dolores' kitchen gave Mrs. Hammond the creeps. It never looked as though anyone was living there, let along doing any cooking.

"If you're going to be here for lunch," Mrs. Hammond said to Joe Dinatorri, "I might as well cook these pork chops and we can eat them. Beats having them just rot."

She went to the phone on an impulse and called up Dolores. Dolores did not have any children. She did not have any house work to speak of because she had a girl come in four days a week. She did not have many friends. And no matter when you called Dolores up she wasn't doing anything in particular. "I was wondering," asked Mrs. Hammond, "if you'd like to come over for lunch this noon with me and Lucy and Rollo and the refrigerator repairman. I got ten pork chops here in my freezer that will be stinking to high heaven if I don't get them cooked and eaten."

"I'll be there," Dolores said.

Mrs. Hammond thought it was a good thing that the refrigerator repairman would be around for lunch. There were times when Dolores spent the whole day in her housecoat without even bothering to get dressed. She would sit in Mrs. Hammond's kitchen drinking coffee and talking about As the World Turns, still in her housecoat at three o'clock in the afternoon. Mrs. Hammond thought it would do Dolores good for once to be up and dressed for lunch.

"You like pork chops I hope," said Mrs. Hammond.

"You got any applesauce?" asked Joe Dinatorri. "I would have to say that pork chops and applesauce is one of my favorites."

Mrs. Hammond liked to cook and Joe Dinatorri liked to repair refrigerators. They spent the morning in the kitchen working.

"Looks like rain," said Joe Dinatorri from behind the refrigerator.

"A real gut buster," Mrs. Hammond said. "That water is going to come tearing down from those clouds and like to wash us all away."

Lucy came into the kitchen. "Rollo says it's going to storm."

Rollo followed her. "And lightning and thunder." He stuck his head behind the refrigerator. "Lucy's scare of lightning," he said to Joe Dinatorri.

"Rollo ate the scab off his knee from where he fell off his bicycle," Lucy said.

"Liars get struck by lightning when it rains," Rollo said.

"Children who don't behave themselves and bother the repairman don't get any lunch," said Mrs. Hammond. "I'd advise certain parties to hush their mouths."

"Do you know how to measure lightning?" asked Joe Dinatorri.

"Lucy can't tell time," Rollo said. "I can."

"Thunder is the noise that lightning makes," Joe Dinatorri went on from behind the refrigerator. "And the farther away the lightning is, the longer it takes for you to hear the thunder. It's a mile away for every second you can count between when you see the lightning and when you hear the thunder."

"I can count seconds," Lucy said. "One-Mississippi, two-Mississippi, three-Mississippi..."

"What if you don't have any seconds between the lightning and the thunder?" Rollo asked.

Joe Dinatorri reached for a screw driver. "I don't know. There's always been time to count, every storm I been in."

The rain cut loose right before lunch--lightning and thunder and sheets of rain storming down. The sky was as black as night. Dolores came running across the yard from her house with a newspaper over her head. By the time she got to Mrs. Hammond's kitchen she was soaking wet.

"I'm drenched," Dolores said. "I just got through having this dress washed and pressed and now it's drenched."

Mrs. Hammond took the soggy newspaper from Dolores and put it in the trash can. "Have a seat and dry off."

"I'm soaked to the skin," Dolores said. "Drenched."

Mrs. Hammond took a deep breath. "Well, go to the bedroom and see if you can find anything of mine to put on." Mrs. Hammond's little square dresses would look a sight on tall lanky Dolores. "I guess something dry is better than something wet. Just take anything that half way fits."

Dolores wandered off to the bedroom.

"You about ready to knock off for lunch Mr. Dinatorri?"

Joe Dinatorri went to wash up at the kitchen sink. "Smells mighty good," he said. "I have always been partial to home cooking when I can get it."

"Why, what do you eat at home?" Mrs. Hammond asked.

"Oh, this and that. But it's been a mighty long time between pork chops." Joe Dinatorri smiled and went to sit down.

Dolores came back from the bedroom wearing Mrs. Hammond's slippers and housecoat. Back into a housecoat, thought Mrs. Hammond. Fate is against me.

Mrs. Hammond served up the pork chops and they all sat around the kitchen table. She was not at all sure that Mr. Hammond would approve of her and Rollo and Lucy having lunch with a refrigerator repairman. Especially after Mr. Hammond had gotten made an Assistant Account Cashier down at the sweet potato factory, he said it was important for them to be friendly with the right kind of people. Mr. Hammond did not approve of Dolores either. He said she was a prime example of low-life. Dolores' husband was in the merchant marine and was rarely home. Mr. Hammond did not approve of any woman who wore a housecoat in the afternoon and lived alone. The truth was that Mrs. Hammond felt a little sorry for Dolores, exasperating as she could be at times.

"Well, eat up Dolores," said Mrs. Hammond. "I been cooking all morning."

Dolores looked out at the pork chops and applesauce and stewed tomatoes and corn-on-the-cob spread across the table. "I just don't seem to have the appetite I used to." She had eaten an entire bag of coconut-chocolate marshmallows that morning.

"The heat'll do it to you sometimes," Joe Dinatorri said. Joe's wife not only lost her appetite in the heat but she lost her energy. She refused to turn on the stove or pick up a broom or fool with the kids or touch him in bed when it was a shade over eighty-six degrees. Joe wished that he could afford a new window unit, something that would put out 10,000 BTU's. For the past six nights he had brought home Kris-P-Kwik Fried Chicken for him and the kids.

Outside the house lightning cracked.

"One-Mississippi, two-Mississippi, three-Mississippi----Thunder! How was that, Mr. Dinatorri?"

"Fine, Lucy."

"I always count 'one-one thousand'," Rollo said. "It's more accurate."

"Would you like some bread for the gravy?" Mrs. Hammond asked. Mr. Hammond did not approve of sopping gravy, but this was only lunch in the kitchen and Dolores was there wearing a housecoat. Mrs. Hammond felt silly putting on airs. And anyway, Mr. Hammond was not there at the moment.

Joe Dinatorri took three pieces of bread.

"Is it hard to cook pork chops?" Dolores asked.

"Why Dolores!" Mrs. Hammond gave her a delighted bulldog smile. "Are you going to take up cooking?"

Lou was Dolores' husband. Mrs. Hammond knew for a fact that at times Lou was not above giving Dolores a whack or two. Not that maybe she didn't provoke it some, being lazy and a whiner, but Mrs. Hammond still thought it was a bad business. She had told Dolores many a time that if Lou ever got to whacking her around just give a whistle and she would run over and personally give Louis something he wouldn't soon forget. Fortunately Mr. Hammond did not approve of husbands who whacked on their wives. But if Mr. Hammond would ever try taking a whack at her, Mrs. Hammond thought it would certainly be the first and last time for such foolishness.

Mrs. Hammond got coffee for them and chocolate milk for Lucy and Rollo. Joe Dinatorri told them a story about the time that he had been called to fix a dishwasher and discovered that a mouse had been caught up inside it and little clumps of gray mouse fur had clogged the works.

"Was there mouse fur on all the dishes?" Lucy asked. "On the spoons and forks too. And mouse guts?"

"Well," said Joe Dinatorri, "let me put it this way. If that lady had asked me to stay and have pork chops for lunch, I think I would have said, 'No thank you, ma'am.'"

Mrs. Hammond laughed. "I can tell you one thing," she said, setting her little mouth in a straight line. "The day you find a mouse in this kitchen is the day I'm not living here any more."

"I found a roach in the Rice Krispies this morning," Dolores said miserably.

Outside the storm was still beating down.

"Hey," Lucy said. "There was barely time to count one-Mississippi, Mr. Dinatorri. Honest, I had just got through with 'one' and then it thundered."

It was about that time when lightening split the big pecan tree in Dolores' front yard. Half of it fell through Dolores' roof and half fell on Mrs. Hammond's front porch, poking one ragged branch right through the kitchen window over the sink, smashing the glass and letting in sheets of rain.

"Oh my God," said Dolores.

"It wasn't even til 'one'!" yelled Rollo.

"That tree," said Mrs. Hammond, pointing one angry finger. "It's in my kitchen!" She glared at the branch, but it didn't move.

Joe Dinatorri went outside to look over the damage. He got a saw from the tool box and cut off most of the branch that was poking through Mrs. Hammond's kitchen window. Lucy cut her foot on a piece of glass. Rollo looked out the window and saw that his brand new bicycle was lying crumpled up underneath the porch railing. Dolores only hoped that the roach in the Rice Krispies was crushed to smithereens when the tree came crashing into her house.

Mrs. Hammond put a bandaid on Lucy's foot. She promised Rollo she would ask his father about buying a new bicycle, although she didn't think Mr. Hammond would approve. He was saving, first off, to buy a sterling silver pen and pencil set for his desk at the sweet potato cannery. And then for a new house in Oak Manor Hills. Mrs. Hammond wouldn't trade for fourteen of those picture-window Oak Manor Hills houses that all looked alike only in different colors. She liked her own little house, even with a tree sticking through the kitchen window. Joe Dinatorri hacked away at the branch and nailed up a piece of plywood over the kitchen window to keep the rain out. He and Mrs. Hammond mopped the glass and water up off the floor. The drying rack full of dishes by the sink had been swept to the floor and most of the dishes were broken. Mr. Hammond would have to wait for his pen and pencil set; he definitely would not approve of eating off paper plates.

Joe Dinatorri sat down at the table to dry off a little. "It's not too bad over here," he said to Mrs. Hammond. "You'll have to have some work done on your porch and get a window put in." He looked over at Dolores. "It looks pretty bad over at your place. Nobody was inside were they?"

Dolores seemed to be staring at them from under water. "I was over here having lunch when it happened."

Mrs. Hammond gave Joe Dinatorri a look. "Well, just who did you think it was eating at the same table with you, Dolores? Let me get you a cup of coffee or something."

"Mama, my bandaid got wet and fell off."

Joe Dinatorri took a look at Lucy's foot. "Why don't you put on another bandaid and some shoes and socks."

"Shoes would hurt my foot," Lucy said.

"How about bedroom slippers?"

"Slippers are too hot for summertime."

"You have until the count of three," said Mrs. Hammond.

Lucy went to get her shoes on.

"I tried to call Eddie to tell him about the tree in our kitchen, but the phone doesn't work," Rollo said.

"Lines are probably down." Joe Dinatorri straightened up his tool box and wiped up some of the water he had tracked in by the refrigerator.

Mrs. Hammond gave a fierce glance around her kitchen. It was dry now and partly cleaned up. It would take more than a tree to get the better of her.

"Drink your coffee, Dolores," she said.

Dolores giggled.

"What, may I ask, is so funny?"

Dolores shook her head. "I can't tell you."

"And why not I'd like to know?" Mrs. Hammond said.

"You'd yell at me."

"I would not yell at you, Dolores."

"Yes you would."

"Try me and see."

"If I tell you, will you promise not to yell?"

"Go on, Dolores," said Mrs. Hammond.

"I'm going to kill myself."

Mrs. Hammond gave her a harried glance and sat down abruptly at the kitchen table. She folded her arms across her chest. Joe Dinatorri leaned against the refrigerator and took a second look at Dolores.

"I am," Dolores said and giggled again.

"I think that is the most ridiculous piece of rubbish that I have ever heard," said Mrs. Hammond in her sweet clear voice.

"Hah!" shouted Dolores. She sprang up and knocked over her coffee cup, spilling hot coffee over the table. She threw the cup down on the floor. She stood blazing at them in Mrs. Hammond's house coat, her knobby elbows and long arms poking out of the sleeves, fists clenched. "You can just watch me do it, if you think it's so ridiculous."

Rollo and Lucy stood by the door staring.

Joe Dinatorri slowly bent down and picked up the pieces of the broken coffee cup. "Maybe if you told us why," he said quietly, "it might help."

"Why?" Dolores laughed. "A goddamn tree just pulverized my house, and my lousy husband is due home in three days and he'll get one look at the house and pulverize me. And he asks me why. Oh that's a good one."

Joe Dinatorri had to admit that things looked pretty black.

Dolores gave them a wild look and darted to pick up a knife off the table. It was a long sharp knife and it was coated with cold grease and pork chop gravy. She stood in the middle of the kitchen waving the knife. "You see this?" she asked them. "You think it's ridiculous?"

Rollo and Lucy still stood in the doorway. Mrs. Hammond turned her fierce little bulldog eyes on Dolores. Joe Dinatorri stood very still and straight in front of the refrigerator.

"You will not do anything of the kind in my kitchen," said Mrs. Hammond. "In front of my children."

Dolores laughed and Mrs. Hammond noted with a sinking feeling that it was more of a bark than a laugh. If there was one thing Mr. Hammond most certainly would not approve of it was Dolores cutting herself to ribbons in their kitchen.

"You know, I remember one time when things looked pretty black for me," Joe Dinatorri said, almost to himself. "It was right before Christmas one year and a piece of pipe hit me on the head and for six weeks I couldn't move my face." He talked on softly, standing motionless in front of the refrigerator.

Thank goodness for Mr. Dinatorri, Mrs. Hammond thought.

"I couldn't move my mouth to talk or eat and I couldn't shut my eyes. At night I had to put my arm across my face to go to sleep. Imagine that, trying to go to sleep with your eyes open. Well of course I was out of work and I couldn't afford to buy presents for the kids and my wife had to go out and get work as a telephone operator. And I was home one day, just lying around listening to the radio because they came and repossessed our T.V., and the phone rang. I went and picked it up, mostly out of habit since I couldn't move my mouth. And there was this voice on the other end that said 'This is radio WDIX and if you can name the song that just played you'll win our jackpot of $478.' And I knew the song because I just finished hearing it on the radio, but I couldn't say anything. So the guy hung up on me."

Dolores shook her head and waved the knife. "Before there wasn't anything *wrong*. There just wasn't anything right. But now there's something wrong. Everything's wrong." She cast a crazy look around Mrs. Hammond's kitchen. Even after the tree coming through the window and the broken glass it was still neat. And organized. When Mrs. Hammond's refrigerator broke, somebody came to fix it. And the cabinets were filled with lots of food. Not bags of chocolate-coconut marshmallows from the dime store. Real food. Peanut butter and crackers and cans of soup and tuna fish. And fresh vegetables in the ice box. There would never be a roach in Mrs. Hammond's Rice Krispies. No roach would dare. Dolores picked up the coffee pot and threw it at the stove.

"Why shouldn't I?" she yelled. "Why shouldn't I?"

It's a sin, Joe Dinatorri started to say. But instead he told her, "You never know when something good may happen. It might be out there, waiting just around the corner. And this way," he pointed to the knife, "you might miss out on it."

"Like when what's-her-name on As the World Turns had amnesia," said Mrs. Hammond. "And then, right at the last minute what happened? Why, she got her memory back."

"You got to stick it out, that's all." Joe Dinatorri said.

"Why?"

"Keep on going," he said.

"Why? Why? Why?" Dolores cried.

"I don't know," Joe Dinatorri said. "But you got to."

"Please," said Rollo in a little voice from the doorway.

Dolores felt all the crazy energy drain out of her. "Oh hells bells," she said and threw the knife down. It bounced off the corner of the refrigerator, cutting Joe Dinatorri on the ankle in the process. Dolores started crying. Mrs. Hammond sat Dolores down at the table. She retrieved the coffee pot from the floor, rinsed it out and started fresh coffee. She gave Joe Dinatorri a damp paper towel and some iodine to put on his ankle. Lucy and Rollo ran to the bathroom to bring him a bandaid.

"We'll just clean up your house the best we can," Mrs. Hammond said to Dolores. "The same as we did with my kitchen. Slicing yourself up is no way to behave."

"I'm tired," Dolores said.

"Here, you take a nap in the bedroom and later when you feel better we'll go have a look-see." Mrs. Hammond left Dolores lying in the bedroom with the blinds pulled, her long legs poking out over the edge of the bed.

In the kitchen Rollo was sticking bandaids on Mr. Dinatorri's ankle. Mrs. Hammond poured a cup of coffee and sank down into a chair.

"Well, I guess we talked her out of it."

"Oh," said Joe Dinatorri, "I think so."

"I declare you were a marvel. A real marvel."

"It was nothing much."

"Is your foot all right?" Mrs. Hammond asked.

Joe Dinatorri smiled at her and went back to his tool box.

The rain had slacked off and quit when Joe Dinatorri had finished working on Mrs. Hammond's refrigerator. He found the leak and patched it soundly. "I don't guess this will be giving you any more trouble," he said.

Mrs. Hammond thought about Dolores asleep in the bedroom. Mr. Hammond would not approve at all if he came home and found Dolores on his bed. Mrs. Hammond took a deep breath.

Joe Dinatorri looked around the kitchen. It was all back in order now. Mrs. Hammond had made tuna casserole and lemonade for dinner.

"Well," he said. "I guess I better be going." He had to get to Kris-P-Kwik before it closed.

Mrs. Hammond nodded. She walked to the door and watched him drive away.

Hotel Roma

Les Standiford

"I'm going home," Beth shouted from the bathroom.

I was lying on the bed, staring up at the ceiling. A water stain had spread out a pale brown outline of Italy. Where Rome should have been, where we were, a chunk of plaster had fallen away, exposing splintered lath and a tiny crevice that led into darkness.

I wondered if she meant it. She wasn't one to make threats. And maybe it would be for the best. Maybe I'd made a mistake, asking her along. I'd also begun to think of earthquakes, of the catacombs that laced the ground beneath the hotel where our tour had put up.

The phone rang then, and the door to the bathroom flew open. She had one towel wrapped around her middle, the other turban-fashion on her head. It made her look exotic. "You're going to get that, aren't you," she said. It wasn't really a question.

I hesitated. There was a flush in her cheeks. I could barely see her freckles. "If I don't, they'll just come to the door," I said.

"We don't have to answer," she said.

I nodded my head, but I wasn't agreeing with her. The ringing of the phone stopped and left a silence in the room. She let the towel slip toward the top of her breasts and cocked her hip at me. "Who's more important?" she said. She could be forgiving. She gave me the smile that offered everything.

"That's not fair," I said.

The phone began to ring again. "Fair doesn't enter into it," she said.

I threw up my hands. "It's my job," I said.

"Then why did you bring me with you," she said, quietly. She pulled her towel up and disappeared into the bathroom.

"That's a dumb question," I called as the door slammed. It was our honeymoon, after all.

Every summer for five years, I had traveled around Europe as an escort for groups of college students, most of them women. The pay was minimal, but it wasn't exactly like work. And I'd been hammering on a dissertation in Art History all the while. The trips gave me access to museums I'd never see otherwise, gave me the sense that I was making progress, that someday I'd finish.

I'd met Beth the previous Fall, at an exhibition lecture in Boston. Rosetti, Hunt, Millais: The Pre-Raphaelites. My dissertation subject. The last, doomed, moral ground of art. She taught painting to schoolchildren.

She'd been standing in front of Millet's "Angelus," the sentimental rendering of a peasant couple pausing from their labors in the field, offering an evening prayer.

"Isn't it peaceful?" she said, turning to me.

Green eyes, a spray of freckles, all that dark red hair pulled back, spilling onto her shoulders. I glanced back at the painting. "It was a simpler time," I said, shrugging.

"Do you think life was ever simple?" she said. Her smile. That unflinching gaze. She knew me.

The rest of the story is familiar: I asked her to lunch; we began to date; before long, I moved in. She taught, I kept grinding on the book.

She'd come home excited, trailing bright sheets of fourth grade watercolors--"Look at this Jack. You could eat that chunk of blue." I'd listen to her and imagine facing my committee, waving my arms, imploring: "Just feel these colors! Take a bite of the ultramarine down there in the corner." But it took me out of the swamp of moralism for a while. She was good for me.

When summer came, I wavered: stay home, finish the degree, be with this woman. On the other hand, there was Europe: intrigue, adventure, freedom. In the end, I tried to have it all. I'd proposed, and here we were, in Rome, on the ropes.

The phone was still ringing, a notch louder, it seemed. I rolled over, the bed shuddering beneath me like land ready to give way. The phone was a relic, with a fabric cord and a ring that vibrated the nightstand.

"Yes," I said, picking up. I expected one of the students. We'd only been checked in half an hour. There was bound to be something: someone's toilet not flushing, the wrong number of beds in a room, something dead in a drawer. I was glad that Beth was in the bathroom. I had been the constant complaining that had done her in.

She was still upset about last night, in Naples. I'd promised her dinner by ourselves at a place overlooking the harbor. One of the local guides had told me about it. There was an American cruiser moored far out in the bay. The ship's lights glowed through the summer haze as if all of Sorrento floated there.

Beth had charmed the waiters with her easy smile and pidgin Spanish. Her hair glistened in the candlelight. They love red hair in Naples. I'd felt happy, even smug.

We were halfway through the pasta course when I got the call. One of the boys had been arrested for shoplifting. I was at the station house until midnight.

"*Professore*," the phone brought me back. It was the voice of the concierge, quivering with anger. "We are missing a key."

I considered it a moment. The older hotels where we'd been staying tended to have just one key for a room. You were to leave it at the desk when you went out. One of the students had probably gone off with it, stranding a roommate outside. We'd been in Europe nearly a month, but our group was a slow study.

Of course, there were other reasons the keys disappeared. They tended to be huge things, fastened to ornate tassels or chained to tooled brass fobs the size of doorknobs. They looked suitable for opening palace gates, and the students favored them as souvenirs. We'd had to hold our departure from Stresa, waiting for one of the boys to "remember" slipping his key into his luggage.

As problems went, this was minor. And though I knew how Beth felt, it was my job to take care of it. I was an escort. An arrangements man. There to make things run smoothly. As one of my colleagues in the escort trade put it, "We're the Metamucil of this screwed-up outfit."

"Don't worry," I told the concierge. "The key will turn up. I guarantee it." The last was a phrase I'd found useful. The hotels disparaged the morals of American students, but if I vouched for the huns, the management would sit tight.

"You do not understand," he said. "I must have the key now. It is an e-mer-gen-cie." I could sense him jabbing his chin with every syllable.

"Look," I said, "let me talk to whoever it is. They can just wait until the roommate gets back. . ."

"It is not one of your students," he said, incensed. "It is another guest. He and his wife are locked in their room and they cannot get out."

. I looked across the room to the heavy door plate. Sure enough, another relic. No lock switch. A massive brass slab with a lever handle and a keyhole. If the door *were* locked from the outside, you'd be stuck.

"Please, *professore*," the concierge was shouting. "The key!" I heard the murky sounds of plumbing from the bathroom, of Beth banging things about. "I'm coming down," I told him. And fled.

"The key was taken from the outer door," the concierge said, confirming what I'd thought. "The cylinder was turned, and *then* the key was removed." He said it the way you'd say 'stuck the knife into the priest and *twisted*!'

I nodded. "I've done that," I said. The concierge gave me a look. "Left my key in the door, I mean." He turned away. We were standing under the hotel's entrance canopy so that he could oversee the efforts of a workman who was raising a ladder against the granite facade of the place. A thin Italian man in a suit and his heavy-set wife were standing at the railing of a tiny second story balcony, staring uncertainly at the ladder as it scraped up toward them.

"The gentleman has an important engagement," the concierge continued.

"Doesn't anyone have a master key?" I asked.

I'd been so naive that he refused even to shake his head. "We could break the lock," he said, grudgingly, "but it would be very expensive."

I nodded. He meant that there were no conceivable circumstances under which the lock would be broken.

By now, the Italian man was helping his wife over the balcony. A young man in the kitchen whites stood a few steps down the ladder, steadying her great ass with one hand, clinging desperately to a rung with the other. He had his head averted as if God hovered just above him, calling down his judgments. The workman holding the foot of the ladder craned his neck, trying to get a better look up the woman's dress. Her husband glared at his watch and shook his head.

"I tried every room on the way down," I said. "But you know how it is. They hit the streets right away."

The ladder shifted slightly on the railing and the woman cried out. The husband steadied the ladder and shouted angrily down at her in Italian. Several pedestrians had stopped to watch and nearby traffic had slowed. A chorus of horns sprang up from vehicles further up the boulevard. There's not much patience on the Via Veneto.

The concierge glared at me, then looked away. "It is outrageous," he hissed.

"You can't be sure it was one of my students," I said. He had thinning hair slicked back on his pasty dome, carmine lips and a weak chin that he used in sighting down at me. I knew what the students were capable of, but I was getting tired.

He spun back upon me. "You have been in my hotel an hour. Who else would it be?"

I imagined hitting him, but the thought passed on. It was hardly the thing an arrangements man could get away with. I turned. The Italian woman stood on the sidewalk, patting her chest with a hankie, watching as her husband made his own way down. She didn't seem anxious about the outcome.

"If one of the kids has the key, you'll get it back," I said to the concierge, but he was already on his way to placate the Italians.

I found the bar in a corner of the vast lobby. It was cool, and gloomy, like the rest of the place, and suitably far from the front desk. I'd thought about going straight back to the room, but the thought of Beth waiting with her "what now" expression stopped me. Worse yet, I might find her actually packing. Instead of commiseration, I'd have problems squared. No, a drink was the ticket.

The bar was done up in white Naugahyde, with some tall ice-cream chairs for stools, and a big round mirror behind, the liquors arranged across its face. There was some dim yellow light that trailed up the mirror from a hidden source and a thin man in a white jacket silhouetted against it, his arms folded.

I thought the bartender was watching me approach, but when I got closer, I realized he had his dark eyes fixed on something behind me. I turned then, and understood. It was Leah.

She was sitting at a small table just inside the entrance, her dark blonde hair pulled back severely and slung in a long braid across her shoulder. She was wearing a black cocktail dress, one stockinged leg crossed atop the other. She was smoking, ignoring the gaze of the bartender, toying with her glass. I had a fact sheet for everyone of the tour members. It said she was only twenty-one, but that's the trouble with statistics.

She cut her glance at me. "Are we drinking this afternoon?" She motioned to a chair. I sat down.

I sat there for a minute, letting my anger burn away. I could hear Leah's cigarette hiss. The bartender showed no sign of movement. I had started to signal him, when she put her hand on my arm.

"Have some of this," she said. There was a heavy green bottle in an ice bucket nearby, and an extra glass on the table.

She reached to pour for me, left the bottle on the table, and slid the glass my way.

"It's Asti," she said, waving at the bottle as if to apologize.

She glanced about the deserted bar. "Fellini would like it here," she said.

I nodded and sipped. The fact sheet told me Leah's mother lived in Hilton Head. Her father listed an address in Manhattan. She'd attended more than one of the sister schools.

"Looks like you were expecting somebody," I said finally, raising the glass.

"You," she nodded. She stared at me, expressionless.

I gave her my arrangement man's chuckle. There wasn't much agreement on the escort's code of ethics, but fooling with the customers was doom on everyone's list. People so far away from home, most for the first time, are basically insecure. They count on you for the maintenance of their comfort as they journey through alien lands. Give twenty-five of them the idea you're sleeping with one of their number, and terrible feelings are spawned.

"You can spot it right away," a local guide from Paris told me once. "You step on the bus and no one smiles, no one talks, no one asks a question." She opened her great French eyes wide. "And oh, how much they complain."

She was right, of course. They become a sullen, defensive crew, impossible to guide through the territories with ease and grace. It is an arrangement man's nightmare. And still, it happens.

I downed my glass. "Looks like you're headed out somewhere," I said.

Leah have me her stare, her aquamarine eyes slightly crossed in appraisal. It was the same look which had set all eight of the fraternity boys with us into endless torments of lust. "Why don't we cut out the bullshit and talk like two people," she said. There was no malice in her voice. No wonder all the girls hated her.

I reached for the bottle and poured my glass full. "Sure," I said. "What would you like to talk about?"

She smiled then, a rare act for her. She had not been sullen, but neither had she been friendly. She'd been with us from Amsterdam to Munich, to Zermatt, to Venice, to Athens, to Florence, to Pompeii, to Rome, interested enough in everything, excited not at all.

I'd seen her modeling a full-length mink one night in a shop on Mykonos. I'd been passing by on the narrow cobbled street and glanced in the open door as she stood before a mirror, clutching the lapels at her throat, coolly assessing her image. Another tour girl stood nearby, watching mournfully. The coat so suited Leah, even the eager shopkeepers were speechless.

She will look like that all her life, I thought.

"Where's your wife?" she asked.

I finished my drink. "In the room," I said. "I had to come down to deal with a problem." I hesitated, then gave in. "She's getting a little tired of hearing about these things."

Leah nodded. "Those people on the ladder," she said. "Weren't they a pair." I didn't ask her how she knew about it.

She sat back and recrossed her legs. It seemed to take a long time. She lit another cigarette and pushed the pack toward me. "You haven't been together very long, have you?"

I shook my head and lit a cigarette. I hadn't smoked in nearly a year, since I'd moved in with Beth. The smoke seemed to explode inside my head and I felt my balance waver.

She blew a ribbon of smoke toward the dark ceiling. "Jesus Christ, I think I'd die if my husband brought me along on something like this."

My head was still reeling. "You're married?" I asked.

She shook her head, amused. "Of course not. I meant if I *was* married." She laughed. "All these people and their *needs*," she said, drawing out the last word.

I shrugged. "It seemed better than leaving her, five weeks together on the continent.

She raised her eyebrows. "I'm sure."

"Plus I get to squeeze in some work on my dissertation."

She nodded as if she knew all about it. "You've been at it a while."

I nodded.

"How come it's taking you so long?"

I glanced at the bartender, who didn't bother to look away. Finally, I turned back to her. "If I knew," I said, "I'd be finished now."

It got a faint smile from her, but she was shaking her head at the same time. "Some honeymoon," she said.

"Hey, it's not like we haven't had fun, or anything."

"Travel is so broadening," she said, deadpan.

She thought for a moment, then trained that gaze on me. "I know what your book needs."

"You do?" I said. I knew it was time to get out.

She nodded, her lips parted.

I felt the wine now. I turned. The bartender was still standing motionless before the yellow orb of the mirror. "I'd like a gin, with ice," I called, my throat thick. After a moment, he bowed, and I heard the clatter of glass. Then, something soft dropped to the floor beneath our table and Leah's bare foot was on my thigh.

I was staring out the window of Leah's room over an endless vista of rooftops, listing antennae, and laundry. The sun was going down in a great boiling of red. There was a set of nail marks across my chest, across one shoulder. Would Beth be gone by now? The city looked to be in flames.

"You've got a nice ass," I heard her say. I knew she was propped up in bed, watching me. She would be lit with the harsh glow from the sky.

"What happened to your roommate, anyway?" I had turned in profile, but I wasn't going to look at her. Studying art, you get to know the old stories. I had a long pull from the bottle we'd carried up.

"She's upstairs, screwing her way through the Southeastern Conference."

I nodded. "I'm thinking this was not such a good idea."

"Get a grip," she said. "I'm no gossip." I heard the sound of a match popping.

"That's not what's worrying me," I said. I traced the shadow of a bird's flight across the dying light. I thought I saw a larger shape swooping down upon it.

"Don't you get tired, taking care of everybody else?" she said.

I thought about it a moment. "No," I said, staring out. "I do other people well."

She laughed, but it sounded angry.

"By the way," she said, finally, "I've got that key."

I turned. I was hoping I'd misunderstood. "What key?"

The light angled across her perfect breasts. Her face was in shadow. Where her hair trailed down into the light, it seemed ablaze.

"What key?" I repeated.

"It's on the dresser," she said.

I stared. There *was* a key there. I pushed away from the window and, as I did, I felt a tremor sweep quietly through the building.

I went to pick up the key. It was for a room on the second floor. We were somewhere on six. "How did you get this?" I asked. I thought of the trapped Italians. I felt very tired.

"You figure it out," she said.

She laughed again, a harsh, biting sound. The sun tipped over and, abruptly, the light was gone from the room. It was stifling with the windows open, and still, I was freezing. However she'd gotten it, I didn't want to know.

I reached down in the darkness for my clothes. "I have to be going now," I said.

"Ciao," she said, as I went out. I did not recognize the voice.

When I got back to the room, I found Beth asleep across the bed, still in her robe. Her lips were parted and her hair was fanned out darkly as if she'd collapsed there. I could see the deep bruise high up on her thigh where she'd stumbled against a chair arm on the bus.

Her bag had been pulled out from the closet, but whether it was half-unpacked or the other way around, I couldn't tell. I was groggy. I thought of Millet's painting, of those trusting peasants praying in their field at nightfall. I imagined a mushroom cloud erupting on the horizon behind them.

I went into the bathroom, cleared some of Beth's things from the ledge above the sink, brushed my teeth, and shaved.

I paused before the mirror. It is possible I spoke to the image there. I was student of art. I was an arrangements man. I had married. Nothing seemed to cohere.

I wanted peace. And still I heard Leah's voice, faintly mocking, "I know what your book needs." There was a groan from the walls, and the floor seemed to shift beneath my feet, as if the ancient hotel had sagged another notch toward all the history beneath it.

The glass in the mirror was cloudy and did not clear when I wiped it. I turned on Beth's hair dryer and aimed it at the glass, but I couldn't get rid of the haze. I set the drier aside, finished the shave by touch, and drew a bath in the huge tub that gripped the tile floor with the claws of a Sphinx.

I filled the tub until I was nearly floating, the water at my ears, lapping the edges. Still, I wanted more of the hot, and I was leaning forward for the knob, when I heard the sound behind me. At first I thought it was Beth, awake at last, and I wondered what I was going to say to her.

I was just turning around when it began. For an instant, I thought the tub was shaking, that the hotel was finally crashing down, but then I realized that it was my own body and not the tub at all. Every one of my muscles had gone rigid. My mouth was frozen open, and I heard myself uttering little gasps. I was paralyzed, unable to breathe, unable to cry out. It was if an enormous hand had clamped down on me and was shaking me violently in the water. I'd cleaned a fish that way, once, over the side of a boat.

The muscles along my spine began to contract, pulling my head back, deeper into the water. I still held to the sides of the tub with my hands, but they were useless, fused to the thick porcelain steel. I willed my arms to pull me up, but there was no response. My vision sparkled, flashed to darkness, then came back again.

I was still bucking, my head going under, when I saw the electrical cord. It snaked down from the socket above the sink mirror and plunged into the water of the tub, near my shoulder. Water was pouring up my nose now, burning, choking me. Yet my mind raced along, unimpaired. The sound I'd heard was something falling.

Then I realized. The hair dryer. Of course. I'd shoved it aside myself, shaving, too close to the edge. It must have turned on as it fell. I could feel the thing now, edging down my chest, my stomach, gliding along like some creature beyond nightmare. "It has a switch for European use, sir." I could remember the clerk who sold it to us. Helpful, helpful, helpful.

My head was all the way under now, my eyes locked open, the light above the sink shattering into dancing planes of light. I felt the dryer balance on the shelf of my groin momentarily, then my body convulsed, and it slid on over into the deep. My head was vibrating against the bottom of the tub. My fingers had begun to quake. A shadow fell across my eyes. How the one in charge dies, I was thinking. . .and that is when everything stopped.

There was a moment of utter quiet, of peace, of time suspended. This was how she'd find me, like that poor bastard we'd seen in Pompeii, a fossil of volcanic ash just trying to do something simple like get out of bed. I wondered what *he'd* been up to the night before it happened.

I imagined the three artists watching from the shadows of the bedroom, pointing at Beth, at me, discussing the composition, the light, the moral implications of the scene. They have arranged it all, I thought. I'd have laughed if I could.

And then, I felt feeling return to my hands, to my feet. A tingling at first, then a buzz, a fire in my lungs.

I burst out of the water gasping, the cord still draped over my shoulder. I glanced up in panic, but saw that I was safe. The plug had separated from the socket near the light. The dryer swirled in the eddies at the foot of the tub.

At first, I wondered if Beth had rescued me, but the place was eerily quiet. It took me a moment to realize: the dryer's own weight had pulled the plug out as it slid down the bottom of the tub.

I heaved myself over the edge and lay gasping on the cool tiles of the floor. When I had finally caught my breath, I wrapped myself in a towel and staggered into the bedroom.

Beth stirred when I sat down on the bed next to her. Her eyes flickered open, stared blankly, then began to focus. She pushed herself up on one elbow. "God," she said, groggy. "Are we still here?"

I nodded. I wasn't sure I could speak. There were a series of dots pressed into one side of her face from the pattern of the spread. She was lovely.

She raised her hand against the light flooding in from the bathroom. She squinted at me, and this time there was concern in her voice. "What happened?"

I thought for a moment. I saw her eyes tracing the marks on my shoulder. We could hear the water draining from the tub. "Nothing," I said, "Just some guy and his wife couldn't get out of their room."

She nodded, stood up from the bed, began putting things into her bag.

"Hey. It didn't have anything to do with us," I said.

She examined a pair of socks, tossed them at me. "I meant it when I said I was going. This is crazy."

"I know," I said. "It's no honeymoon."

It's no honeymoon," she said. She laughed, but didn't mean it. She glanced at the open door of the bathroom, then back at me.

"You can't have everything, Jack."

"I don't want everything," I told her.

She looked at me squarely. "At least be honest with yourself."

Then, the phone began to ring. Beth glanced at it, went back to her packing. It gave me a moment. I was an arrangements man. An expert at smoothing things over. The thing with the hair dryer was a gift, a happy accident. Tell her I almost died, she might forget the rest.

There was an ancient print on the wall above the phone stand. Fuseli. Darkness at the fringes, bright flesh at the center. A demon crouched on his lady's breast. The incubus leered out at me. I could feel the silk clutched in his hairy toes, the pulse in his veins. You're with *me*, he nodded. We'll eat your artists up.

The phone rang on.

"Aren't you going to get it?" Beth said, over her shoulder.

I hesitated. She pulled on a shift and hoisted her bag. The artists hovered in the shadows, disgusted, ready to pack it in, head back to their own century.

The phone had shifted to some higher key. This was life, imitating art. I'd studied *art*.

I reached out suddenly and yanked on the phone cord. It was strong, but it was old. On the second try, it finally snapped, sending a little burst of plaster up from the wall. The Fuseli print crashed down behind the bed.

"What are you doing?" Beth said.

"Let them work out their own problems," I said.

She stared at me, surprised. After a moment, she put her bag down. I took her hand and told it all. I prayed she'd lean my way.

The First Prayers for Me

Jeff Todd

The bottle of Pepe Lopez tequila still sits on the formica kitchen bar, its miniature sombrero cap adorning my salt shaker. But I left the sliced lime out overnight. The wedges are shriveled at the middle and browned. In my refrigerator between near-empty jars of Hellman's and mustard I find a ReaLemon, liquid concentrate in a plastic lemon container, authentic down to the fake leaves. I could buy an actual lime at Winn Dixie, but I don't get paid until Monday. Besides, I'm tired after cooking all day and don't want to drive. What the fuck. I snatch the ReaLemon and slam the fridge door, pushing to make certain the seal connected.

Joey said he'd have my VCR ready this evening. He's only charging ten bucks to replace the head. I treat him right at Waffle House by loading ham and green peppers into his omelet. I don't do that for everybody. Joey fixes stuff, Teddy at the distributor gets cheap cases. Except for the occasional lady who smiles pretty, with everyone else I'm careful. I add just the right amount of ingredients. It's not right to do it any other way; I could get fired.

After licking the crescent between my left thumb and forefinger, I sprinkle salt. I pour tequila into my Zoo Atlanta shot glass--the only one not chipped--and set the opened lemon to my right. Lick, shoot, squeeze. The jet sprays the back of my throat. I learn that ReaLemon is far more sour than the fruit. Still, not bad for a first run. For the second shot I mix a minute bit of concentrate directly into the tequila. It tastes better.

6:30. Joey probably isn't finished. He doesn't like rush jobs because he makes mistakes. I can't stand talking to his fat wife Emma who flirts. She wears sleeveless shirts and her arms are the size of my head. Every time I go over she wants to play cards. Sometimes hearts or rummy, but usually spades when her fat friend Jo Lynn is there. They eat Oreos and kill us since I seldom play. She owns decks from all the Biloxi casinos and talks about her scheme for blackjack. But when she goes every other week she only plays quarter slots. To pass time I drink more tequila. The bottle is near-empty and doesn't fill the glass. I slam it anyway; a half-shot's better than no booze at all.

Todd

Even though I need to drive, a beer with dinner wouldn't hurt. I open an Old Milwaukee to go with the sausage and egg sandwich from work. After eight hours over the grill, a cold beer is necessary. I down half of it standing before the fridge and grab another in case the first empties. My brown-with-checkered-sleeves polyester work shirt stinks from sweat, grease, and wiped-on condiments. I chuck it toward the bedroom before sitting in my recliner. The left side dents down and the foot rest sticks, but for 12 bucks at the Salvation Army, I don't complain. I place my food on the scratched end table and lift the remote. It hangs in the Armchair Quarterback bag, a Christmas gift from my ex-girlfriend Tina.

Without cable the channel selection blows. That's why I need my VCR. I only pick up four stations, and one of them's a televangelist network. It's a load of shit. I watched one time, and this guy with big hair said that someone in the South was hurting, and to send a donation so he could pray to God and end the pain. He might have meant me, but I don't have any money. I bought the TV cheap from Joey; a customer never picked it up from his shop. So I said the Rosary that Sr. Claire gave me in fourth grade. She said to make heaven work, talk to Mary. I prayed for her to perk me up and smoke the evangelist. I felt better for awhile, but he's still on the air.

Star Trek: the Next Generation is on Fox. Even though I don't understand the jargon, I enjoy the big Klingon and Riker who does all the chicks and the breasty brunette. I settle my beer on the Quarterback Coaster and eat the sandwich. It's lukewarm, but that's all right. Like every episode, this one focuses on a ship-wide problem that could mean death for thousands, and a personal difficulty for one crew member. That's how I'm different from *Star Trek*; like when Tina broke up. Even though it sucked for me, all of Mobile was not endangered. I'm kinda glad she's gone; she was expensive.

I finish the sandwich without touching the beer. Work makes me so hungry I gulp food. I chug my brew and open the second. Those real-life police programs are on now. After the show I'll pick up my VCR, make sure Joey's done. No point in rushing him. I watch some cops in ugly brown uniforms pull over a drunk driver and give him the business. That happened to me once, but I passed the roadside sobriety test with menthol cough drops. I'm more responsible now; I usually drink close to home.

Before the middle commercial break I finish my beer. I drink the remaining one from my case. Joey can wait until 9:00; he's probably not even done yet. Maybe he'd doing big Emma. I sure wouldn't want to interrupt that. Seeing her naked is more than I could tolerate. On the way to the bathroom I pick up my shirt and toss it onto the hamper. It hangs, caught on the broken plastic. Brown streaks the tile where the caulk's bad on my tub. I piss holding the can in one hand and my dick in the other. I wonder if the next swallow could drop down and exit with the current flow? I sprinkle on the floor and decide to take a quick shower.

After emptying my pockets onto the sink counter, I hang my clothes on the doorknob. Not much there: three keys, a near-empty wallet, and my Rosary. Even though I haven't attended Mass much since I switched to public school, I still say the Rosary. Sister Claire made me do a paper on it. I learned everything, from its foundation of prayer beads and the introduction by St. Dominic, to all the Mysteries and proper technique. Always when I feel sick I say it, but only for other people. Sister Claire said personal requests were selfish. The shower has to run hard for the plug to stay up, but I don't pay water so that's O.K. Steam takes the food sweat off, then cold to cool down. During our last argument Tina said I drank too much. I pray the Rosary for her still.

After a long shower I rub the thinning white towel all over, extra through my hair. My sister Jean told me I should pat-dry to care for my skin, but that takes too long. Besides, my skin's trashed from 50-hour-a-week exposure to bacon and sausage grease. I'm constantly washing my hands and arms; otherwise, they break out. Nobody at work gives a shit. They just want a continual supply of prepared food. Customers are worse. They order crap like bacon-and-egg biscuits then complain because it's too oily. I wipe on Gilette Sport Stick, five swipes per side, and a splash of Drakkar. I throw my towel over the curtain rod and drop my clothes into the hamper.

I take the beer and walk naked into the bedroom. Thinking about Tina gives me a semi. I gyrate to the theme music of the next show on FOX, flopping around. I think about shooting a load, but I need to save strength in case my neighbor Leila comes around. She's Baptist, always talking about God and inviting me to church, real religious. She has a bod for sin; I think she's interested in the humpty dance. Since Catholics drink and Baptists fuck, I'm hopeful. I spend my free time watching TV, so the bedroom isn't much--a single bed that's never made, a thrift store table, and a dozen plastic crates from Waffle House. A giant neon green tapestry of Springsteen hangs at the foot of my bed. I choose a pair of loose-fitting boxers, proper TV attire. The tapestry cost only four bucks; I don't much like The Boss. I could do a Rosary for him, pray his music gets better.

I drink the Old Mil dregs, but I'm still thirsty from work. An almost untouched fifth of Jim Beam calls for use, so I mix half-and-half with 7-Up and plunk in some ice. The Thirst Buster cup is kind of huge, 44 ounces, so I'll wait until 11:00 before I visit Joey's. Right after the *Saturday Night Live* News, when the show goes downhill. Joey stays up late anyway, and then I can visit only a second and not deal with Emma.

The recliner thumps back and sets. Because the Armchair Quarterback Coaster is too small, I rest the cup between my legs, right hand gripping the handle. Maybe I drink faster when I hold a glass this way. The show is another real-life cops, except now they're in New Orleans during Mardi Gras. There's a police chick who speaks German or Russian and some mounties, like at Langan Park near the University. Most people don't even know Mardi Gras started in Mobile. Tina told me that. Her parents are into Mardi Gras balls and parties, spending monster dough on costumes. They're not even Catholic. Usually I just watch the parades from Teddy's window, which is almost on the route, and drink beer with Joey and him and some of his friends. We don't catch anything, but we also don't get shot. Then I go to Ash Wednesday Mass where Fr. O'Henry thumbs a burnt palm cross onto my head. I always give up something bad for Lent, like last year chocolate and the year before corn chips.

By show's end I've finished the bourbon and seven. When I stand my vision slants, so the room's not parallel no more. With my hip I smack the barchair but catch myself. Got a good buzz going. I only mix a half-glass so I can still make it to Joey's by midnight--zip in, pay, and zip out. No fat Emma. I say Rosaries for her, too, that she'll lose weight, so Joey can screw her without that big belly in the way.

At 9:00 I surf through the channels. There's a police drama and woman show and some made-for-television movie. Because of the Mardi Gras cops I hum "Second Line;" one of the marching bands in the background played it. I always imagine the New Orleans Saints cheerleaders when I hear the song. Tina and I attended a ball once. I'd never seen so much booze and food--beer, call drinks, wienies in sauce. She drove home. Now I'm hungry, but I don't have any munchies.

I rummage through my shelves. Behind a couple dead roaches, which always die on their backs, I find a box of mac and cheese and can of peas. Out of milk, I go with the peas. A saucepan of congealed water sits in the sink. I dump it, rinse, and scrub with the steel wool. After wrestling the top off, I pour the peas, which shlork into the pan. I want to make sure they're cooked through, so I set my timer at 10 minutes. The kitchen floor's not as solid as the rest of the apartment; I feel myself rocking forward and back. I drain the peas through a vented spoon. They're so plain I don't taste anything when I try some. A mound of butter and every seasoning I can find--salt, pepper, paprika, and nutmeg from Christmas--add enough zest.

To view the TV I stand at the bar and eat straight form the pan. The spices burn my mouth, or maybe bug spray stains the fork, so I gulp the drink. That Mardi Gras show keeps me thinking about Tina. She was wrong. I should call her and say so. I barely remember all seven digits so I let my fingers dial. I tell her she was wrong. I'm not an alcoholic loser. She has the problem and needs some help. I say I'll pray for her. A woman that sounds old tells me I must have the wrong number. I probably do. At work sometimes I mess up the orders, like instead of no tomatoes I add extra. Dumb shit like that. I say I'm sorry and hang up. Since I can't remember Tina's number I'll call her tomorrow, except I'll write down what to say.

I can feel the peas burning down my throat. They start to churn in my stomach, like after I eat a whole pizza. To soothe the fire I want more liquid, but I don't move for a moment. I burp and it hurts. The TV and recliner start to spin, and my stomach goes with them. As fast as I can I walk to the bathroom. I can't hold it in. I throw up in the toilet, on and a little around it. The peas are still single units, even though they're mushed. Then the alcohol smell hits me, mixing with that gray-green slime, and I hurk again. I drop to both knees. The back of my throat grows sore when I puke the third time. There's nothing left but I continue wretching. I pull the Rosary from the sink counter. The crucifix sticks behind the toilet paper roll but I yank it free. The names I normally pray for flood my mind, yet I can't focus on one. Fuck it. The first prayer's for me.

"In the name of the Father, and the Son, and the Holy Spirit. Amen."

SUN UP, SUN DOWN

Trellie L. Jeffers

Black folks in town look at each other, whisper, wink their eyes or exchange significant glances when he passes by. Old Miss Sarah, whom folks claim to be close to ninety years old, is blind in one eye, and the sight is foggy in the other. But she sees him, and she spits her snuff through her spaced teeth and grins to herself. Young folks who are now old folks used to talk about it at their social gatherings--church picnics, missionary meetings, church revivals. They either got bored from talking or they became ashamed of dealing with the same subject matter. But every time Dower passes them, they can't help thinking, and reminding the people next to them that they are thinking. So each gives a signal to the other, and if there is no one present, each gives a signal to oneself.

His mother called him Dower. Now, everybody calls him Dower. It was a peculiar name since most black folks in town gave their sons nicknames like Buster, Bud, or Junior. Of course many males received their nicknames from some type of idiosyncrasy or achievement or amiable quality. So Lefty, Shorty, Slim, Sport, Red Hot and the like were the common nicknames. And many got nicknames that were facsimiles of their real names. Dower didn't fit any of these categories. Unlike most nicknames this one was slow to stick. Black folks would therefore roll it over their tongues and then expel it quickly as if it were a type of distasteful food: "Dower, what kinda name is dat, boy?"

When Dower was a small boy, he became accustomed to having to defend his nickname--"What yo name, boy?"

"Do--Wer"

He had a squeaky voice as a boy, and it remained with him as a man. Unlike the black boys in· town his voice never grew thick and husky. This was an additional topic of conversation--

"What you say yo name is, boy?"

"Do--Wer."

"Why you talks lak dat? And whur you gits dat name fum?"

But Dower had already vanished. He spoke little to anyone, answering only the question concerning his name. And this was an

91

answer that his interrogators already knew. In fact folks already knew
his history, for it was a small rural town and most folks knew your
business sometimes long before you did.

"Hey, May Belle?"

"Hey, gurl."

"You heah 'bout Mis Susie boy, Bud?"

"Naw, gurl, whut he don dun?"

On the main street in the major shopping area, there was a block
which all black folks on their way to and from the white folks'
establishments--kitchens, yards, farms and other businesses would be
obliged to cross. Main Street divided the black side of town from the
white side of town. To get to any point outside the black community,
one had to cross the Block. It was here that one could learn both black
and white folks' business. Black folks got up early so that they could
spend time on the Block in order to engage in malicious gossip before
reporting to work.

The sawmill hands, the factory workers, the construction workers,
and farm hands who had lived in the country drove their wives into
town for domestic work. These husbands arrived long before the white
folks stirred and returned long after the evening meal. This gave the
wives plenty of time to spend on the Block to swap tales of other folks'
business. In this manner, the city folks got the country news, and the
country folks got the city news. Dower was the headline of many Block
"news" stories for many years.

These were the same folks now, old and retired, living on public
assistance, who threw significant glances as the middle-aged Dower
passed.

Folks knew that Dower's father had died when he was a small boy,
leaving Dower's mother with six mouths to feed, seven with her own.
Dower was a small child when he experienced this tragedy in his life.
With all the crying and screaming over the dead man, Dower became
very frightened and after the first night, he crawled in bed with his
mother in order to dispel his fear; he had rarely left since, except for
brief periods.

Dower was eighteen when one of his older brothers had an occasion
to call on the mother early one morning and had been horrified to find
that Dower was peacefully sleeping in his mother's bed.

The angry brother had grabbed Dower by the nape of his neck while
the mother calmly watched, dragged him to his bed and threw him in,
cursed him and dared him to share his mother's bed again.

Dower remained calm throughout this ordeal, and as soon as he heard the brother's car pull out of the yard, Dower rose swiftly, neatly tidied his bed and hastily returned to his mother's bed.

In his own house at breakfast the next morning, Dower's brother discussed his shock of finding his mother and his grown brother sharing the same bed.

"She is ruining him, making a baby out of him," the older brother complained over his grits and ham. But the wife had another version of the incident in mind. She didn't dare tell her husband that his "news" was in fact no news at all. For she had been a maid before marrying Dower's brother, and Miss Sarah Ann, the next door neighbor, had long savoured the Block with this spicy item.

"I fixed him," the brother bragged.

"Whut you do?" the wife inquired, feeling compelled to make some type of comment for fear of exposing her prior knowledge of Dower's sharing his mother's bed.

"I thowed his butt outta dere!" the brother bragged.

"Yeah," replied the wife. "You ain fool nuf to thank dat gon stop it, is you?"

The brother looked bewildered, too bewildered, in fact, to pursue his wife's comment. He turned on his breakfast with a certain ferocity. And the wife smiled to herself secretly as she poured him his morning coffee.

The draft in the Second World War separated Dower from his mother. Lonely and desolate, he went off to the Army.. Upon arrival at the Army camp, his first order of business was to take out an allotment for his mother.

After a few nights at camp, he wrote to her:

"I has truble sleepin'; I sho miss home."

After a while the mother, too, became lonely and she decided to take a job in the white folks' kitchen to pass away the time. Her job, of course, took her past the Block amid curious stares and vicious gossip which she either dismissed or ignored.

She was a small woman, frail in appearance and pale in color. She was bent long before old age, and therefore she kept her eyes glued to the ground as she walked. She wore her twenty-two inches of kinky hair streaming in several pigtails down her back.

She barely ever spoke, never socialized, and had little or nothing to say to her other sons and daughters-in-law. So her manner of social behavior made it possible for her to pass through the indictment of the Block and remain detached.

At the rich white folks' house, she did her work well. When she returned home evenings in the summer and spring, she tended her flower and vegetable gardens, or sat on the porch until dark approached and read old papers and magazines which she brought with her from the white folks.

In the fall and winter, she sat in her house and made quilt patterns from old rags, or she crocheted or knitted or sat idly until time to go to bed.

She meticulously saved the money she gathered from Dower's allotment and bought the small house that she had rented from the largest white landowner in town. Later, she purchased the property adjacent to hers.

Meanwhile, Dower's vision of home and his mother began to grow farther and farther away. So when one of his Army buddies suggested to him one night to go out girl-hunting, Dower accepted the challenge with only a slight hesitation. They were stationed in France, and Dower found a warm, silent girl that was his for a night. Until this experience, Dower had never known hunger for the warm body of a woman, and through this woman's initiative, he learned the feeling of having his blood vessels swell and then explode in rapture.

After the first night, Dower went looking each night until he found this woman. His nights with her began to make Army life for him satisfying.

With his French girl, he forgot about the perils of fascism and thought only about getting to the crucial moments with "his woman."

When he was transferred to the Philippines, he quickly found a golden brown woman and though she spoke no English and he spoke no Spanish, the passion was the same.

When the war was over, and Dower headed for home, he had left his brown girl weeping in the doorway of her shack, begging Dower to take her with him. But Dower's heart was already racing home to find another girl, for circumstances had taught him that all girls held the same ecstasy.

When Dower returned from the Army to his small town, he was amazed to find that he had only to look a few houses away from his mother's to find the young woman that he had dreamed.

She was an independent woman who defied society by buying and occupying a house alone. She was a short, shapely, plump woman, the color of mahogany wood, with a mass of thick, kinky hair piled high on her head. She had soft, moist, dark brown eyes that looked earnestly and probingly with deep concern as she spoke. Her tender objective mode of behavior had made her job as the only black waitress in the exclusive white restaurant in town a profitable place of employment for her. When she walked, she moved her firm, large hips with grace: she was poised among the well-to-do customers, and they tipped heavily. Her snow-white uniform (which she wore both on and off her job) always crackled under the heavy starch.

Dower had met her one evening by accident when he sat on the porch as she passed, on her way home from work. He had simply asked if he could walk with her, and she had been straight-forward in answering: "Yes, you may walk with me if you like." Dalmita, it was rumored on the Block, had spent two years in college; some said that she had even taught school before moving to this little town. She had, moreover, impeccable speech and reputation.

After the first evening upon meeting Dalmita, Dower always hurried home from his job at the aluminum plant, took a bath and waited on the porch for Dalmita in good weather and by the window in rainy weather. He would go home with her, do chores for her, eat dinner with her and remain until late at night. It took Dower only three or four months to decide that he wanted to spend his life with this woman.

To Dower's mother's chagrin, Dalmita and Dower were married in an elaborate church ceremony (for a small town) for which Dalmita paid. This of course added a new news item to the Block.

"Yo'all hear 'bout Dalmita and Dower gittin married yestidy?"

"Yeah, chile, wonder how de ole lady took it?"

"Gal, I ain studin 'bout you! But dey say dat she don lak it a bit!"

"I reg not!"

Dower's mother remained silent, absenting herself from the wedding ceremony, and secretly preparing to add this daughter-in-law in the despised category with the others. Even before the wedding, she privately hated Dalmita.

The first three years, Dower's and Dalmita's marriage was seemingly both happy and prosperous. Dower's job as a factory worker and Dalmita's job as a waitress enabled them to save money, to furnish their house (which Dalmita owned) rather elaborately with television sets, plush sofas and easy chairs and even china. And Dalmita's artistic, expensive taste raised envious eyebrows from the other in-laws. But

Dower gave her freedom to buy whatever she wished, for, after all, she had already eliminated the expense of buying or renting a house.

Dower was very satisfied with Dalmita, and he even began to move out of his hermit state. He joined a church and attended with Dalmita; she was an ardent church worker. He learned to play a little poker and began to give and attend poker parties which were played more for fun than money. He, at Dalmita's insistence, joined the Masons and the church choir, and black folks became sure that marrying Dalmita was the best thing that he could have done.

"Yeah, chile she don got him ackin lak folkses."

"He ought to dun been ma'd her!"

Then Dalmita had their first child, and while she lay in the hospital recuperating from childbirth, Dower became frightened by this new dimension in his life. After two nights alone he went back to stay at his mother's.

Upon the return of his wife from the hospital, he sensed a change in his life. He was not sure what or where; he was sure that an important ingredient had disappeared. In these first years of his marriage to Dalmita, he had gone by to see his mother during brief periods, perhaps to fix something or to see whether she was all right. Now, he prolonged his visits, sometimes even staying for dinner. He would sometimes rise early in the morning to go by his mother's and he would come by every evening.

At first, Dalmita did not complain. She would only insist that he take care of his home responsibilities. And Dower would oftentimes stay up all night after coming home from his mother's to fix something in his and Dalmita's home.

When the first baby was six month's old, Dalmita became pregnant with the second. When Dower learned this news, he panicked, and rushed to his mother's house where he spent the night; after this, he began to spend additional nights there.

His frequent overnight stays at his mother's altered Dalmita's behavior. Instead of the soft, sweet-spoken, tender person that she was upon her marriage to Dower, she began to nag and complain bitterly.

She was no longer sweet-smelling, starched and immaculate; she often smelled of sour milk and baby vomit and stale urine. She was fat and her stomach never flattened from the first baby before becoming poked out in her second pregnancy. Her hair was often unkempt and her clothes dirty and soiled. All of these changes had taken place since Dower spent seventy-five percent of his time away from home, for during Dalmita's first pregnancy, she had been beautiful and happy and always filled with excitement.

Now she washed diapers, tended to her first child, and never seemed to catch up with these chores in order to put he house in habitable condition. Before the baby, Dower had always been unselfish in helping Dalmita with the housework; now, he never lent his service, and if Dalmita asked for his help, he sneaked out of the house and went to his mother's. Moreover, Dower had never held the baby, had no idea how to change a diaper or to give it a bottle. For all of this, Dalmita bitterly complained and rebuked him.

When Dalmita went to the hospital to have the second baby, she moved the first baby in with a sister-in-law until she returned from the hospital, and Dower moved in with his mother. A brother-in-law and his wife picked Dalmita up from the hospital: Dower had never gone to the hospital to see her.

Dower's brothers went to their mother's house to try and shame him into returning home. When this failed, they tried to frighten him by telling him that his wife was planning to divorce him unless he returned home. This was not entirely untrue, for Dalmita had decided while she was in the hospital that she would return to work as soon as the baby became old enough. The mother never spoke in favor of Dower's returning home. When Dower had his first pay check after the second baby's birth, he went down and deposited his signed paycheck in Dalmita's mail box and sneaked away.

The second baby was three weeks old when Dower came back home and spent a night. He offered no explanation. He simply came in one night, got a plate from the cabinet and got something to eat. When he finished, he left the plate on the table and went into the living room and turned on the television, watched for a while and then went into a bedroom separated from his and Dalmita's and spent the night.

When Dower rose early the next morning to go to his job at the factory, he found all of his clothes packed neatly outside the bedroom door with a note that read:

"Since that is where you stay, you take these clothes and go to your mother's house and don't come back."

His heart leaped. He felt unburdened. He had not meant to stay at his mother's; he just needed to recollect himself. But as time went by, he was compelled to stay. Something inside of him would not let him go. Now, he sat down by the door and buried his head in his hands. Something had happened to him, and he could not understand it.

Women were no longer appealing to him, not just his wife; all desire for women had vanished. In a way, he thought, his wife had relieved him. Now, he no longer had to agonize, to make excuses to himself, to feel guilty. He took his clothes and left. After three weeks, Dalmita hired a sitter and returned to work. She obtained a quick divorce from Dower and in five years bought a big, modern, brick house for her and her two children.

Every payday for twenty-five years, Dower received his paycheck, cashed it, divided it into exact equal portions and took half of it to Dalmita's mail box.

For twenty-five years, the Block thrived with news about Dower, his wife, his mother, his children...

Dower's mother died last spring and Dower buried her, sobbing uncontrollably as his ex-wife looked on in disgust at a man weeping shamelessly in public and before all of the town's news carriers. Dalmita wanted to go up to him and slap shame into him, as she watched the spectators pinch each other and give signs to each other right in front of the opened casket.

Now, the middle aged Dower, pale and bent like his mother long before his time, walks with rapid paces, even though his back is bent. Each day, no matter what the weather, an hour before sundown when there is sun, or weltering the storm if there is a storm--whatever the weather, Dower can be seen going to the cemetery to spend an hour at his mother's grave. As he passes each day, the children stop their play to observe when they are able to play outdoors. Otherwise, they peep from the windows and observe him rapidly moving toward his mother's grave. They look in awe and confusion until he vanishes from their sight. But the old folks gossip, grin, mumble to themselves or shake their heads and wonder...

First Words

Erika Corey Turner

I started to tell him no, but he pretended he did not hear. Then I screamed: No, no. You're hurting me. Get off. Get off of me. I couldn't believe my voice didn't carry beyond my own hearing; the only proof I have that it carried to the top of the trees was that shapeless messenger-- the transient echo, translating back to me, word for word, my fright. It could not help me, though, and was as scared as I.

I am young, but do not feel my fifteen years. Soon, perhaps, I will begin to rejuvenate my current, yet mythical age brought on by his black-hearted nature. A blunt image of white cruelty, porcelain fat shaped his sides, weighing me down while he thrust inside. One more push. His open hand came down across my face hard. Stoning me with his tongue--words young Indian girls hear a lot--*stupid red whore*. I threw up tears first, then blood. I gave up for the next few moments. I think now that helped save me. I wonder how he can hate so much of the beauty and wonder that lives outside his inner-self and live with the hostility that crawls furtively inside the foulness of his skin.

Right now, I think I know what I want, even if my parents don't agree. I am telling you this because you won't judge me. You are red. A few days ago I tried to peel the skin off my wrists with a straight razor. Today, I regret that and hope someday you will understand it was not you or myself I wished to hurt--but the miasma of all the moments I have been thrown. I long to hold and protect and save you from this coiled snake jar we live inside of. With a few holes in the lid. They tell us we are free. Someday, you may think this is an exaggeration. But, baby, it is true. I am very scared to go through with this. Even more so, I am afraid to lose you and never know life outside this hurtful world I inhabit. You have words attached to your life that are more pure than any other life. They are raw, powerful, untouched, and redeemed. You bring with you the strength to sustain and survive against people of all (un)faiths.

It is only two weeks since that incident, but when I sit here in my room, on my bed, with legs crossed and hands clasped lightly over my stomach, I feel you moving inside me, responding to what I am saying. This story may not be something I will ever tell you at bedtime, but it is real and what I know, and has given me your precious body wrapped inside the maternal pillow of my womb.

All I feel is tied to that moment. My biggest fight now is to untie the moments without losing the one I need to keep. The only one that matters. It is said that beauty is often created in times of chaos. You probably know something about that for you were conceived at a turbulent hour.

Oh baby, don't leave me in this world alone. The breath of your life just sprayed hope upon the surface flesh of my stomach. I am not whispering this, but sending you my voice through the messenger in my heart's mind. It is he I trust, and I will teach you that is all you will need. I only wish I could open my mouth and tell you this, but I am afraid they will hear me, *us*. I still haven't told them. About him or you. All I know is I will not take no for an answer. My child, do you hear me? Can you hear your mother's first words--to you?

He Doesn't Know Me

L. Jean Gardner

Late afternoon was Laura's and my time during our week-long September retreat to Gulf Shores. This Friday we nibbled hot beignets oceanside. A breeze began to dry our damp hair and dusted powdered sugar onto softly faded sweats and the gray wooden bench on the boardwalk. I felt calm. Our union seemed not of our own making, but of one already joined and simply flowing through us like songs the ocean breeze blew against our balcony windchimes. Laura looked and acted twenty, though a playful child within. She gazed down at her feet and bubbled over with little giggles. A tiny mouse peeped up between the boardwalk planks, reaching for the sugar crumbs. I quickly drew my feet under me, fearing the mouse would touch my bare toes.

"Feeling safer now, Mom?" she asked.

I was about to own up to my fear, when I noticed something moving in the distance. The sunlight hurt my eyes as I looked across the water. And then, the circus began! One, two, three, then five leaping dolphins began shooting up out of the water like fireworks. A baby dolphin joined the display in erratic little bursts. Its underbelly looked pink, perhaps from the reflected sun. I could feel their carefree joy as I watched.

I pulled the hood of my sweatshirt closer around my neck, snuggling down. I chose to live in this moment, protected from thoughts of her leaving the next morning.

She looked toward the water as she began to speak, almost thinking aloud. "You know, I really appreciate all that you did for me in high school. I said terrible things." She finally caught the wisp of her thick black hair that the wind was blowing and anchored it behind one ear. She turned toward me. "I was just so angry...especially at Dad...and you got it all...my anger at you and at him."

Her senior year had been at Mountain Valley High School. "It was a hard time for both of us," I said. "Remember the night you decided to move out because you said I would never change? I saw that book of apartment listings in the greater Denver area laying on your bed and knew you were serious. I remember yelling at you, "it's not true that you can't teach an old dog new tricks! We can work this out. I've never given up on you; don't you dare give up on me!" Only three years ago.

101

She lifted her long legs up onto the bench and crossed them in a practiced yoga position. She slowly rocked side to side, and I knew she was adjusting her weight equally. I had watched her do that a hundred times. She finally spoke: "That was a turning point, Mom. You accepted my age; stopped nagging me. . .about my curfew. . .grades. . . getting to work on time. You finally listened."

"You know, Laura, you looked so upset at times, and yet it was hard to know when to nudge you to open up and when to respect your need to be left alone." I had felt such anguish that Friday night, and was utterly lost about what to say or do, the target of her angry, dark eyed glances. I felt afraid. I didn't know how to draw her close.

"At least we both recognized the crisis, and knew we were about to lose each other. I'm grateful that we didn't give up. I guess if we got through that one together, we always will."

Laura pulled her legs up and put her arms around them, resting her chin on her knees. "Dad never listens to me, or takes any responsibility for what he says, or does." She knitted her thick, black brows just as she had in high school until her friends told her how mean she looked. "He just wants to deny any problems, write checks, and then brag about this daughter, the successful political science major. Now that I see him for who he really is, our relationship is improving. But he doesn't know me...how mad he makes me! He'll never know, because he refuses to listen to anything about himself! You do, and that helps."

My daughter was talking about healing. The scar would follow her into her future. I took a deep breath to hold back tears forming in the corners of my eyes. I reached over and held her hand.

A bittersweetness shivered up my spine, and I decided to walk alone to the water's edge. Leaving Laura behind me sitting on the bench, I stepped down the gray wooden steps and felt a familiar roughness under my bare feet. Stepping into the warm, fine white sand I began to struggle as each foot sank deeply into its loose softness. I walked toward the damp harder packed sand, thinking about the continuing struggle that followed me out of a divorce. I had waited so long for an end that I now knew would never come. Her father and I would be united until death because of his importance in her life. I would continue to regret the cost to her. We had only peeled off the outer most layer of the onion, and I was resigned to go with her to the core. But this would be the work of her own life. I could only be faithful and present when called upon.

Finally I reached the harder packed damp sand, and began to walk lighter, more freely on its firmer crust. I was reaching the glassy sea, sending foaming edges toward me in big lazy swirls. I heard birds calling to me overhead. I stood by the water's edge. Soggy wet sand accepted my weight, my footprint. A blue heron swooped down to land on the vacant beach. The bird glanced in my direction, then distanced to a tree top. Eyes directed out to sea, the bird stood still and smooth, like the hood ornament on a classic car. I shielded my eyes with my hands, determined to see what its departure from the tree might bring. I waited. Waves continued to bubble and wash over my feet, and I felt myself sinking unevenly into the sand. Then the bird stretched ever lengthening legs, neck and head. Powerful wings expanded and moved into the air flow, lifting, lifting, lifting. My eyes followed the heron as it continued to lift and soar, becoming a dark speck above the vast Gulf still sending back waves to the shore.

Crystal's Ball

Scyla Murray

Crystal was not conceited, only convinced. As a BWOM--Black Woman on the Move--she possessed the self esteem needed to prevail in a white dominated culture. But it was a world she had long ago chosen to live and work in. And long ago she learned to manipulate and enjoy it. All in all it wasn't so bad. It was more amusing than hostile. Saturday nights Crystal arrived at the Super Mac by 9:00 to obtain a barstool beneath the flourescent Emergency Exit sign. She had a perfect view of every *man* who entered the front door. More important, each had a clear view of her.

Tonight Crystal chose to wear her hair pushed back with a neat slick line of baby hair framing her face. A red amaryllis jabbed into the tiny bun was the exact color of the lycra dress with bare shoulders she bought on sale at the Korean shop at 63rd and MLK. She wasn't supposed to buy from *them*, but when Mrs. Wong threw in the expensive red stockings that come out of the egg there was no saying no. After all, a bargain is a bargain. Crystal had borrowed her friend LaQuitia's red Pucci shoes which were a little tight and hard to dance in, being 2 1/2 inch heels, but every BWOM knows that heels make the legs ir-re-SIS-ti-ble. Earlier that afternoon Crystal got a French Wrap with REALLY RED nail glaze to match her lipstick. The monochromatic look is never out of style.

For the bartender, eyeing her out from the other end of the counter while arranging and rearranging the peanut trays, Crystal examined each of her long fingers under the red light from the Exit Sign, the gold *C* pendant dangling from her right pinky like a crescent moon. Then, pulling out a departmant store tester of Venus D. Milo cologne from a small red purse, she placed her index finger directly behind her ear and slowly traced the natural line of her jaw to her naked collar bone. Careful not to smear lipstick on her teeth, she bit down on her lower lip, tilting back her head so the bartender could watch the tiny red beads on her earrings brush along her shoulder. Now, you put the "F" in fine, she thought, reaching for the bar menu.

Crystal had conquest on her mind and considered what drink would accomplish the task. Shall I drink beer? A pitcher is cheap but no man would approach me. A person who wears a tool belt and boot cut jeans to work orders herself that and I do not want to be mistaken for you know...one of them or worse, with someone. Maybe a glass. No, he would know I drink it in the can at home. Tap beer attracts a man who habitually goes for pizza and bowling on a date, possibly the 1.50 movie--not *this* sophisticated diva. Crystal crossed her legs, readjusting her skirt, and spied an FYM--Fine Young Mandingo--at the door. A light beer is too saditty. I do not want him to think I am conceited. He would appreciate me solely for my ravishing beauty and style, not the entire package. White women drink that stuff and it doesn't even taste. The only foreign beer Crystal could pronounce was RED STRIPE and she knew it was Jamaican. A BWOM never settles and I am not *even* prepared to deal with the cultural gap we have with those "Coconuts."

Crystal never ordered colored drinks. That catagory included Blue Hawaiians, Pink Ladies and Orange Surprises or anything with excesses of sugar, umbrellas and fruit kabobs. Wine coolers and pretty drinks attracted the *wrong* men: manipulative machos, two timers and wife beaters. Sighing sensuously--in case an FYM happened to be listening-- Crystal recalled Elliot; he talked to her a couple months ago. She met him while drinking a Blue Devil. Not only was he secretly married, he was insanely jealous and had a nervous twitch. He called her every hour, cased her home, and had the nerve to follow her to work. Finally, Crystal broke down and borrowed a sawed-off shotgun from LaQuitia's brother Lamr. She only had to show the gun and he left her alone. Crystal don't play. Sweet drinks and pretty drinks advertise an inferiority complex--easy to manipulate and childish. Men know that women drink to hide the taste of the liquor. "I drink to fit in so abuse me." Frozen drinks were equally bad. A tease, sweet yet frigid. Rapists and serial killers wait for a girl drinking a magarita or pina colada in order to have and excuse to commit a violent crime. Crystal was too savvy for that situation, no matter how fine the man.

A glass of wine or martini would catch a lawyer tonight; just enough to attract someone shallow with a steady cash flow. A real wine lover would never pay $3.50 for Gallo's. Tonight, thought Crystal, I think I want to meet someone who is "legit." A gin and tonic, rum and coke or screwdriver would lure a man able to handcle a BWOM. Mixed drinks are simple and signify a woman with internal strength and intelligence. Sometimes what is most obvious is most mysterious. Crystal looked down the bar, and by putting one peanut in her mouth at a mouth time tried catching the bartender's eye. A mixed drink was four dollars. That is quite a bit of money, especially when someone will buy me one. But, you can't catch a fish without a bait. "A Perri-air with a twist of lime." Water *looks* like gin and is only 1.00. Not a bad choice, thought Crystal, tracing her lips with her tongue; and then when offered a drink I could get what I *really* want, a double. As the bartender put down the drink, Crystal slid a dollar bill across the counter. Putting her elbows on the table to show her cleavage, she looked directly into his eyes, winked--cautious of her mascara--and smiled in lieu of a tip.

Machismo

Jim Sanderson

Even now, though I am over forty and a veteran Border Patrol Agent, chicanas still call me "pretty boy." I think they mean a good-looking, light-skinned, promising chicano boy. My ex-chicana-lawyer-girlfriend said, it was because I had a young person's want was in my eyes.

My mother, an anglo, called me "pretty boy" too; but she didn't use the term like a chicana. She would face me into a mirror and say "look at my pretty boy." My mother's angular anglo lines made my face. I was light-skinned, *un güero*, like my father. I've got my mother's green eyes and my father's thick black hair, now with a lot of gray.

When I started to school, my father's pretty boy good looks and my mother's anglo lines had not yet molded my face. I had the fat cheeks and straight black hair of any *mestizo* boy. So for the first day of school, at the end of August in Brownsville, Texas, my mother dressed me in a coat and tie from her father's store. She knew that the other kids would stare at me while I sweated and tugged at my tie, but she also knew that they'd know that I was white or at least that I had her, a classy, rich white woman, as a mother.

The only battle that Miguel Martinez ever won against my mother was naming me. While she was out under anesthesia-back before natural childbirth recorded by husbands with VCRs-my father, with a delicate, looping script, right under my footprint, wrote *Adolph Miguel Martinez*. When he read that his grandchild would have the same name as Hitler, only with Anglicized spelling; my grandfather, Charles Beeson, the owner of the Beeson chain of clothiers, wanted to shoot ol' Miguel for the second time in his life. But murdering in-laws was something that Mexicans did, not prominent Anglo Rio Grande Valley citizens. My grandfather helped bring the touring opera companies to the Valley and always bought season tickets. He gave to fashionable charities and tried to start a minor-league baseball team for the area. He was twice elected to the Brownsville City Council and had a Brownsville city street named after him.

The first time that my grandfather wanted to shoot Miguel was right after his daughter told him that she was pregnant by a "Mexican." The wonder to me was why Sandra Beeson, a member of the privileged anglo aristocracy, a girl who could have chosen any boy she wanted, especially a prized anglo boy, let this trashy Mexican in the leather jacket stick his dirty hand into her panties. This *pachuco*, this hood, this aging hispanic teenager, was probably bound to be stabbed or thrown in prison. Then I wondered why she would marry him. There were, of course, even in those days, plenty of solutions. Maybe she took a secret delight in plunging into the backseat with the type of boy she was supposed to stay away from. She must have had a good time pissing off Chuck Beeson. And back there, sometime during my conception or shortly after their marriage, or maybe around my birth, she must have loved him somewhat or somehow.

The Martinez's, I understand, were happy to see Miguel married. A wife might calm down their troubled boy. And marriage to this rich *gringa* would lift Miguel and his children into the type of social position they enjoyed in Mexico but could never have in the U.S. My father's middle-class people ran away from the Mexican Revolution and settled in the Rio Grande Valley. While learning to speak English, they slid down the social scale but retained their educated atheism.

And Miguel must have strutted for a while after he "scored" with the popular *gringa*. He might have felt a little of the Hispanic machismo that comes with getting a woman pregnant. He might have been a whole lot scared at suddenly getting married and giving up loafing and speeding with his *vatos*. But he too, at some point around my conception, or maybe around the marriage, might have loved Sandra. But by the time I was born and became "Adolph" and then spared from that name by my mother nicknaming me "Dolph," they had started fighting.

Charles Beeson tried to clean Miguel up. He bought him a suit, gave him some credit at his department store, and tried to teach him the correct way to pronounce English words. He gave Miguel a job as a suit salesman and had hopes to promote him first to the manager of the mens' department in one of his stores and then to a manager to of an entire store so that his wife and grandson could have the type of life they deserved as their birthright.

But Miguel didn't work on his accent, his manners, or his salesmanship; instead he drank more. The day my mother bundled me up and moved out; my grandfather fired my father. Even Miguel's own parents disowned him for blowing his chance to jump up some social rungs.

My mother insisted that she take some kind of job in order to support the baby that her father was more than willing to support. So Charles gave her Miguel's old job. And Sandra led the department in sales, and then became the men's department manager, and then store manager, and then took over Charles' business. And just before the malls completely destroyed her family's heritage, she sold her small chain to a bigger chain of discount department stores.

I met my father on one of my walks home from my first year in junior high. I walked along an irrigation ditch and was still young enough to be interested in the frogs that gathered in them. Sometimes, I'd slide down the banks, getting dirty the clothes my mother still picked out for me (still, slacks and dress shirts, though I began to talk her out of a tie), and stick my hand into the tepid, stagnant water and try to come out with a pet frog. He'd only remain a pet until I got him home and lost interest in him or my mother threw him out. Other than the frogs, I liked to lean my head back to my shoulders and gaze up at the tops of the palm trees, which were planted in rows to serve as property markers, while I walked under them and imagined myself standing still and the palm fronds passing over me. I was doing this when my father saw me.

"Hey, kid," he said, and I brought my head down to see a scrawny man eating a bean burrito and drinking a Falstaff beer. He squatted next to his pick and shovel. His dirty, sweaty T-shirt clung to his chest and stomach, and sweat dripped down his forehead, off of his nose, and onto his burrito. "What you doing?"

"Looking at the palms," I said.

"Looking at the 'palms,' not the 'trees,'" he laughed. "*Son los arboles las palmas*. You got it, *las palmas*," he said. "You a smart boy. You know where they come from."

I shook my head, "From Spain and North Africa. I bet your momma don't tell you that."

"*Hablo Español?*" he asked. I just stared at him.

"You speak Spanish?" he said and hung his head.

"No," I said.

"I guess your momma won't let you?"

As young and as surprised and as curious as I was, I didn't like him picking on my mother, "She says I should, for business. My grandfather says I shouldn't worry about it. Let them speak English."

Miguel put his head back and laughed, then he pointed the neck of the beer at me, "You learn to speak it. You speak it, you'll be an important man. *Muy macho*, huh?" He nodded as if asking if I understood.

"I don't have to listen to you."

He got up and pushed out his hand with the burrito in it. "You want some?" I shook my head. He offered me a drink of his beer. I shook my head again. "Yeah, you too young to drink much now."

"I could drink."

He poked the bottle of beer at me again, and he laughed when I grabbed it, took a big sip, and grimaced to get that first taste of the luke-warm, bitter, metallic liquid down my throat.

"Maybe next time, I give you a coca-cola," he said.

"What next time?" I said.

"You come by here after school. I'll be here."

"Who are you?" I asked.

"*Yo soy su padre, muchacho.*"

I cocked my head to look at his sweaty, sun-dried face. The sun had darkened him, but he could still be considered *güero*. Then I looked down at my arm; he was not as light as me. He smiled with both his eyes and mouth, and I could see remnants of that pretty boy, *pachuco* hood. And in his eyes and nose, though he seemed ancient at the time, I could see myself, what I am now, though he was aging faster than I am now. Evidently, his genes were a lot stronger than my mother's; all I got from her was a lighter complexion and blue eyes. "You mean you're my father?" I asked.

"*Sí*," he said.

We didn't talk much after that, and I grew nervous and started to move past him. He scared me when he reached out to take me by the shoulders and look me in the eye. "Maybe you won't come back," he said. "Maybe your mother won't let you see me. Maybe I won't be able to find you no more. But some things, sometimes, you got to do for yourself. You understand?"

I nodded though I had no idea what he was talking about, "No, you don't know. Sometimes you got to go against what your mother and your grandfather say. Okay? *Muy macho*, huh?" he said.

And I left him to his shovel and pick, to dig out the dirt, rocks, and trash blocking the irrigation ditch. I later learned that clearing out blocked irrigation ditches was one of the odd jobs he picked up when he was sober. Thus began my meetings with my father.

Sometimes, when he'd walk home with me, just far enough toward home so my mother wouldn't see him, we'd pass Our Lady of Mercy

Church, and he'd make me cuss the church, and then God, and he'd tell me not to expect anything from any God." The first time I said the awful f-word that my mother told me never to say, I said it just before the word *Jesus*. I didn't feel like I would be struck down by a bolt of lightening or that I would roast in hell; in fact, my father Miguel Martinez said, "See there, what did God do to you;" I felt nothing at all blasphemous, but I felt ashamed that I had said a nasty word that my mother wouldn't approve of. After that, the words *goddamn*, *mother fucker*, and even *chinga tu madre* entered my vocabulary, and I made more friends with the boys at school.

On one of my later visits with my father, Miguel took me to a *curandera*. She scared the piss out of me at first. She had a lazy eye, so that you couldn't tell if she was looking at you or lost in some trance and staring off at God. She turned over tarot cards and told me that I was going to face great trials in love or some other vague shit that anybody could figure out. Then, to protect me, she sold me a charm: a special candle to burn at nights.

Miguel waited for me outside of her shack, and when I came out, he put his hand behind my back as though to help me walk across her dirt yard, but I really knew that he was trying to steady himself. As we walked down her *barrio* street, only kids in dirty diapers and their mothers out at this time of day, all of them staring at the drunk loafer and his son, Miguel moved his hand to the top of my shoulder so that I could better steer him. When he saw a scraggly mesquite, the only tree in this dusty, dirty, dried-out housing division of tar-paper shacks and discarded lumber, he steered me to it, and we both sat down, while he mopped at the sweat on his face.

My mother would have been incensed had she known that I was in this neighborhood with the low clotheslines so that sheets and towels almost hit the dirt, with the stray dogs that sniffed at everybody, and with the open tin drums used to burn trash, little alone that I had just been to see a *Curandera*. Of course, at the time, just as I was starting high school, I couldn't figure out that corrupting me or just getting me to do something that would piss off my mother was my father's real motive.

"What did you think?" he asked.

"Not much," I told him.

"Good, good," he said. He dug in his pocket and pulled out two cigarettes. One had already been lit and charred. He offered me the whole cigarette. I shook my head because my mother told me not to ever smoke. Besides, I didn't want to spend my spare change on cigarettes.

"What's the difference between that old witch woman and the Catholic Church?" I shrugged my shoulders. "See, you got it right. None. Worst thing to ever happen to Mexico was the Catholic Church."

"Why?" I asked.

"Never, mind, I tell you later. This ain't the point." He frowned as he looked at me as though to discover the point. "Oh, yeah, yeah. What's the difference between this old witch woman, and whatever church your momma takes you to?"

"She takes me to St. Luke's Episcopal Church."

"Don't matter which one. What's the difference?" I shrugged again. "See there. You are a smart boy. Ain't no difference. They're all the same."

He pushed himself up along the skinny trunk of the mesquite and tried to stand even though some of the limbs were in his face. "Remember, religion is for weak people. A man don't need no religion. He looks at things the way they are. He don't need some old crazy woman, priest, or preacher. Religion takes away dignity. It don't give you none." He tapped his chest with the flat of his hand then he put out his hand, extended his forefinger, and shook it once.

"What?" I asked

He shook his hand once again, and I gave him the candle that the old *curandera* had given me. He threw it on the ground and stomped it with his heel. "She said that would be bad luck."

"Fuck her," he said.

"Okay fuck her," I said. "But what about the things the church teaches? Like forgiveness and grace and mercy, compassion, sympathy." He had already taught me to cuss the church and shoot the finger, so he was no longer shy about cussing around me or I around him. He liked to hear me cuss. When I wrapped my lips around a *fuck* or *goddamn*, he probably had visions of his corruption of me, of my growing up to be some sort of successful and rebellious misogynist like him.

"Fuck them, too," he said.

"Naw, you still need those," I said.

He looked at me and weaved a bit as he held on to the tree and moved a limb out from in front of his face. Then he smiled, "okay, okay." He hesitated while I stood up, and he patted my shoulder, "Now you starting to think for yourself. Pretty soon you don't need no Papa."

"Okay," I said and started to back up. "I've got studying to do."

"Hey wait," he said. "You think I give you these lessons for nothing. I even paid for that old witch to read your future."

I had begun saving my lunch money or giving him some of what I made from my own odd jobs or summer jobs-bagging groceries, cleaning up my grandfathers' stores. I pulled out my billfold and unfolded my two crispest, newest dollar bills and handed them to him. "Get something to eat," I said.

"You a good boy," he said, then looked back at me to smile, "No, you a good man."

My catechism with my father also extended to women and beer. He bought me my first six-pack and helped me drink most of it. He gave me my first sip of tequila. And, of course, he was the first to take me to the boystown at Matamoras. He insisted that every boy, "no every man" (he deemed me a man when I was seventeen, a year earlier than the army), needed to knock off his first piece at a whore house. "A whore knows what to do. She shows you good," he said.

I didn't like the smell or the impatience of my whore, whom my father picked out and I paid for. She was a young woman with a Caesarian scar, and I didn't like the way she held my tool in her hand, washed it, then idly said, "Okay." Maybe, it was a bad pick, but she was my first and only whore. Perhaps, I should have tried again.

And afterwards, with my father slumped in a chair in the cheap bar, a couple of strippers serving drinks, a few college boys clapping and hooting, and an little man with a dainty moustache announcing, in English, the arrival of "the monkey," my father gave me my lesson. "So what was it like?"

"Okay," was all I dared to say. I didn't know whether to fess up that I was little scared and a whole lot embarrassed or whether to boast that I slammed it to her.

"That's all?" He slapped the table and tried to straighten up in his chair. "It should be. . ." His mind got cloudy, and he couldn't finish his sentence.

"It was. It was. It really was great," I said and smiled.

"Good. Remember that." Then he put his elbow in the middle of the table and leaned toward me. His tequila breath hit me and nearly knocked me backward. "Don't ever confuse that with no love." I nodded. But he shook his head, "No, you not so smart, smart boy. You don't understand. What if some *gringa* you go to school with comes up

113

to you and says to you--no, no comes to your momma and says 'Dolph made me pregnant'?"

While his finger waved in front of my face, I tried to second guess what he wanted. I mostly wanted to be home in the safe, civilized world of my mother. By this time, he had stopped being amusing and was mostly annoying. I guess I went with him because I felt that I ought to. I gave my mother's response to his question. "I'd set down with her and her family, and with mine--my mother and grandfather-and decide what was best for all of us."

"No," he slammed the table with the flat of his hand. "You get out. You run away." Though he was drunk and impatient with me, he must have seen the shock or hurt in my face. After all, even though I had just had my first piece of ass, I was still mostly a child. "Well, no, no, not really," he said. "What I mean is you can't let no woman control you." He squinted his eyes and exhaled as he thought, and a smelly but invisible cloud of his breath hung in the air. "What I mean is you decide." He planted his elbow in the center of the table and pointed at me firmly with his gnarled finger, "What I most mean is a woman is fine for fucking, you know. And maybe that's all. But you don't let nobody have your life. A woman comes up pregnant, you run like shit."

His eyes came together. He said some more, but I couldn't understand his words. I nodded my head though I really didn't know what he was trying to tell me, nor if he had any clear idea. But I helped him up, and we sloshed through the mud of the Matamoras boystown, refused the drugs and sex toys of the street peddlers, until I could flag down a taxi.

On the way back to Matamoras, my father passed out. I drug him out of the taxi and paid the driver. As I tried to drag him around the square, a couple of Matamoras policemen tried to question me about the drunk. The only Spanish I could think to say was "*Mi Padre*." They looked at me suspiciously but didn't take either one of us to jail. I couldn't carry him across the bridge into Brownsville, and even if I could, I had no idea where he lived. So I left my father on a park bench in the Matamoras square closest to the U.S. border, and I walked home. I saw him again the next week, and he thanked me for taking care of him.

Soon after, my mother found out that I was meeting him. She had heard rumors of her "pretty boy," going to Mexico, walking some bad streets with an old drunk. She forbade me to see him. To make sure that he was out of my life, my grandfather put a peace bond out on poor ol'

Miguel. So when I had my application to Rice University accepted, I turned it down, just like a stupid greaser would do, and joined the army. I didn't see Miguel again until his funeral.

It was winter, and just his parents and I watched the city bury him. Ol' Miguel had been drunker than usual on one of the coldest nights in the Rio Grande Valley in a decade. On this cold night that did years worth of damage to the citrus, ol' Miguel tried to stagger home to the shack he then lived in. He must have known that home was somewhere along the irrigation canal in the little *barrio* where he took me to see the *Curandera*. He had a bottle with him, so he sat down on the irrigation ditch and took a long drink, or so the police guessed. When he got up and tried to stand in the loose dirt of the ditch, he slipped and rolled backward into the cold, stagnant water. He was lucky he didn't drown. He clawed his way half-way up the ditch and simply passed out. Wet, out in the open, in a place where nobody ever dies of cold, Ol' Miguel froze to death.

By the time he died, I was out of the army, out of college, and in the Border Patrol, and I could finally speak Spanish. It was my hardest course in the Border Patrol School in Georgia.

Hawk of the Night

Ewing Campbell

All right, you moonshiners, long haulers, insomniacs, road cruisers, hot-wire artists, and reuniacs that was Thelonious Monk 'Round Midnight' going out to my friends on the Tex-Mex Express somewhere in the night and you're listening to XE *Anno Domini* again, that's XEAD, your clear-channel, souped-up Hawk of the Night, coming to you on one hundred thousand killer watts of our electromagnetic tide, straight up the ether chute from Saltillo, Mexico, high in the Sierra Madre. High, I said. High on your dial at fifteen-twenty kilocycles. And high on that list of what you been waiting for. It's all down-hill from here, clear to Milwaukee, Duluth, Sault Sainte Marie, and beyond. If you're hearing me in Newfoundland, right now, Reykjavik or environs, drop me a card so I can send you free of charge my life-size picture that glows in the dark.

"Now grab your knobs and feel that vibratory affinity. Twirl those cat's whiskers, tweak those tuning crystals, and watch your Leyden jars light up with sparks. We'll be here till three, and you can tell them tomorrow you saw it all on the radio.

"Let's go to the first caller. Eagle Pass, how's that signal there? The ozone skip effect in good order? We're not fading in and out, are we? No static or interference?"

"I--I can hear you."

"Can you hear a pin drop? Are we that clear?"

"I can hear you fine."

"You have something to get off your chest, young lady?"

"It's just-well, the Detrichoma I'm taking. My grandmother ordered it from you because she wanted the steak knives that came with a year's supply. I had this fuzz--"

"You *had* facial hair, right? And needed a depilatory. That what you're trying to say?"

"I--don't know that word."

"Your grandmother wanted a hair remover for you."

"She was anxious to get the knives and said she'd try to do some-thing about the hair at the same time because the waxing didn't work."

"Waxing? What's that supposed to mean?"

"The hot wax was to take the hair off after it cooled and was lifted from my face. The beautician said so, about he wax, I mean."

"Didn't you get the Detrichoma along with the cutlery? The knives? They arrived all right, didn't they?"

"She got the knives--and the medicine."

"It worked, didn't it? It removed the unsightly hair?"

"Yes--"

"What's all this talk about hot wax then?"

"The beautician put her up to it. Said the fuzz'd come off too when the dried wax was peeled. That was the fashion. And after the mucilage didn't work, grandmother was ready to try anything. That's why she waxed my face. But it scalt me and left the skin peeling."

"Let's get this straight for the audience. We're talking about molten paraffin? That's what she used on your face?"

"It was supposed to work."

"But in your case, the skin came off instead of the fuzz?"

"Something went wrong."

"That's when she gave up home remedies and ordered the Detrichoma? We're on same page now--am I right? She ordered our treatment and put it to use? Hello? Are you there?"

"I'm here. Finally she did."

"And you said it worked?"

"Yes--"

"Come on, you night owls. Be constructive. Show some fortitude. If you've got good news, speak out. Don't be shy about it. If the glass has water, say it's half full, not half empty."

"It took off the fuzz. I don't have any now, but my lashes fell out. And my eyebrows, they disappeared. Also my body hair and what was on my head. Then I puffed up. The headaches started. My vision got blurry. I am still swelling. And I don't know what to do about it. How could I when I don't even know what went wrong?"

"Sounds like you didn't follow the instructions."

"She doubled what it said on the label. If half as much is good, she said, then twice as much is twice as good."

"Is your grandmother there?"

"She's here in Eagle Pass, but--"

"But nothing, put her on."

"She can't come to the phone."

"You overdosed. Listen, stop using that product right now. Don't touch it again. Am I clear?"

"Yes."

"Send three ninety-five--cash, check or money order--and I'll see you get a supply of Corputrim. It's the only fat re-ducer on the market with nothing but organic ingredients. All the others have a synthetic diet suppressor or toxins that produce unwanted side-effects. The active ingredients of Corputrim are thyroid extract and bladder wrack. It'll get rid of that swelling or your money back. And by the time you're down to your regular weight, your hair will be back glossy, better than ever. That's a promise, and we keep our word. Give us a ring when you've got good news to report. Let's take another call.

"Hello, you're on the air. What prompts this terrible summons? Come on, speak out. Just can't sleep? Or the heebie-jeebies kept you up? Careful what you say now. You know everything that goes up in the stratosphere must converge, circling the globe forever on the cosmic drift, only to appear later in your gold fillings and over the party line when you talk to the preacher or get wiretapped by your ever curious government. So don't say it over the airwaves if you can't stand by it when the sun comes up."

"What?"

"You heard me. Tell us why you're calling."

"Hawk, here's why I'm on the horn to you from out in Hondo."

"Hondo? That the town with the mayor--Glasscock what's his name--wants to give the feds back their money?"

"The same, Hawk. It's Woody. Woody Glasscock's the mayor, but what I'm calling for is--"

"What's your name, Hondo?"

"Call me Hank from Hondo, and I just want to say I'm up at this hour because my vigor's not what it used to be. I'm too tired to sleep. And the marriage--well, the marriage is suffering."

"Your conjugal vigor, Hank? Am I getting the gist? You not quite the same old Sancho was tupping the flock at twenty? That your concern?"

"Things don't happen like they used to is what I mean."

"We can talk around the bush all night and not get anywhere, but if you want the straight stuff, I've got the world's leading authority on the subject speaking by remote from his Hill Country Clinic in Del Rio, Texas.

"Doc, are you on the line? Old darling Hank from Hondo needs a straight talker, and I'll bet he's not alone out there. Can you tell him and the folks at home something that will ease their worries?"

"Indeed I can. A little plain talk never hurt anybody. Fact is it's saved many a life and marriage. If it's a question of sexual weakness, the answer to the problem is right at hand. Provided, of course, this is not an ailment due to domestic indiscretion."

"No way, Doctor."

"Your complaint, then, is in all probability a result of diminished testosterone."

"What?"

"Testosterone. The hormone produced by the male reproductive glands. The reservoir gets low as a man grows older. It's a common problem, but one which a skillful thaumaturgical procedure can correct. It's simple, safe, and guaranteed to restore you to a higher energy level than you had before your capacity got to this point."

"Hold on a minute, Doc. Are you saying Hank can be a better man than he was when he was at the peak of his virility and not taking a back seat to anyone?"

"I'm saying he can be twice as good as any man in Hondo, Texas."

"Well, don't hold back, Doc. Tell the caller how."

"If the caller will just come over to my clinic in Del Rio, Texas, that's the Hill Country Clinic, I can transplant traces of Toggenburg testes. It'll be over the same morning, and within forty-eight hours or shortly thereafter, he'll have as much pep as he had at eighteen, if not more. You've got my guarantee on that, and we'll put it in writing. He'll get a certificate of warranty, guaranteeing satisfaction or his money back."

"Are you talking about goat glands, Doctor?"

"I am. There is a testicular coincidence between the Toggenburg and *Homo sapiens*. These traces grow in the human body without rejection. My anastomotic technique taps right into the energy of the host. We've conducted blind clinical studies and the scientific data show--"

"But goat glands?"

"Slivers, Hank, cullion traces, nothing more. Hear what Doc is saying. The studies show what, Doc?"

"A ninety-six percent success rate. And when we go back to see what happened in the other four percent, we discover, through state health records, that the patient's not been forthcoming about past indiscretions. Throw out the moral transgressions and we are right on a perfect one hundred percent rate of success."

"Beeper's going crazy. We got more callers trying to get through, Hank. Doc, stand by for any other medical question that might come up. Modesto, you're on the air."

"Hey, Hawk, love what you're doing."

"What's your question, Modesto?"

"I just called to say my ex had Doctor's procedure four years ago after we tried the longest without success. It transformed him. That billy goat needed dehorning afterwards. Now I have two sets of twins and another kid thrown in for good measure. It's better than fertility drugs or conventional enhancements. Truth is I got more than I bargained for."

"Thanks for the testimonial, Modesto. I'll add some news here, straight from the trade papers. Says one Farley Reyes out in Frisco is taking his 'Bay Talk' national, going coast to coast--a hundred and forty-nine new stations across the Great Divide on the Continental Radio Network. Congrats, Farley. Way to go. While the little guy worries about half a hundred stations in the central valley and northern California or another twenty-five throughout the Old South and up the Atlantic coast, giants like Farley are opening up new frontiers.

"Closer to home and even more ambitious, Houston radio station KODA announces in a press release it's expanding its international scope by broadcasting the 'Brent Clanton and Jerry Hudson Morning Show' from Tokyo. Just imagine the view from there, and you saw it all from the very front row.

"What does this signify? What are they doing out there? I'll tell you what it means. They're trying to catch the old Hawk of the Night and XEAD because we've been international all along, the big one in the sky, your own international Hawk of the Night. What's two hundred or so Continental Radio Network affiliates when you're hitting every town and hamlet, big city and farm place in America? If you've got a radio, you've already heard us. If you've got a radio, that's why you're listening right now. What's a new network pick-up when the world's your audience. When you're going out over the airways of XEAD with the Night Hawk, the whole world listens. Meanwhile, let's hear it from Smithville."

"Hawk, I can't sleep nights, worrying about my water."

"What's the trouble, Smithville, blood's in your stream when you make water?"

"Make water? No, our drinking water's what I mean. And my irrigation. Have you heard about salting the Colorado?"

"Not that I recall. What about it? Which Colorado's that?"

"The one in Texas and I'll tell you what about it. LCRA's been lax on chloride levels in the river."

"LCRA? Listen up, you night birds. Don't take anything for granted. Spell it out."

"The Lower Colorado River Authority, which allocates water from the river for my fields. When I irrigated the peas this year, the plants turned brown and died in a week. Got to be a sideshow before it was over. Neighbors driving by to look at the sight, stopping long enough to commiserate with me, saying it was a shame and there ought to be a law. I lost the whole crop, and now, the land might be ruined too. The bilge they gave me is brine and watering with brine is like plowing salt into the soil. But what's really got me scared is the drinking water. And I'm mad as hell about it."

"I expect you are. Okay, if you'll just explain it to the audience and be concise we'll get right to the bottom of this."

"Right. Well, it's oil wells. The brine in those unplugged holes contaminating the ground water and in some cases the surface water. The problem is it's getting into the river. We take our drinking water from the river, and the blood pressure of everyone in the family has gone way up. To a point of concern. Our homestead's important, but the family health is more so."

"What you need, Smithville, is one of our bacteriostatic water treatment units and adapters for the irrigation if you're going to make a crop next time and enjoy the full flowering and profit of your labor. Here's how it works. The Edwards Aquifer Pure Water Corporation's filters and reverse osmosis system will make delicious, safe drinking water that is free from sodium. It forces water molecules right through a semi-permeable membrane by mechanical pressure, thus removing dissolved contaminants from the water. All of them. Salt, arsenic, lead, heavy metals, you name it. Removes them all. The system was developed by the U.S. Government to make sea water potable.

"But that's just your first step. You and the family are sick right now as a result of what's been done to your water. So you need to order a six-month supply of Coahuila Water Crystals to purge your system and the family's of that high blood pressure and any bloating that might accompany it. Do not wait. College professors, chemists, scientists, and medical doctors swear by this product which, by the way, is derived from distilling the richest mineral water known to man. In the process, water is converted to vapor and carried off, leaving only a healing essence in the form of pure crystals. Just stir a spoonful of crystals into a cool glass of your Pure Water three times a day with meals. That's morning, noon, and night. Drink it down slowly and you'll lose that bloated condition right away. Your color'll come back. You will be regular and your health will be totally restored. They cannot take your health away if you don't let them, folks. Go for it, Smithville. And the rest of you, too.

"All right, night birds, let's cue up a Bud Powell piece for your musical pleasure. We'll be back shortly with some important announcements and take your calls for more late-night conversations with the Hawk. We've got the lines, and they're all open. Just give us a call. Hold it. I've got a light winking at me. Cedar Falls, you're on the air. How do we look from there?"

"Just pathetic. The girl that called earlier. Any more like her and that's it. I won't listen. I can tune you out or not."

"Sorry you feel that way."

"I mean it. There's no place for a creature like that on the public airwaves. I know a bad conscience when it raises its ugly head. You can hear it in her voice. The Bible says--"

"Now, lady, don't be truculent. Play fair. What does the Bible say?"

"I can't quote chapter and verse, but it says the sins of the fathers shall be visited on the children. Brothers with sisters. Fathers with daughters. Mothers with sons. It's not natural, girls with hairy faces, men with breasts and hips. Morphodites, Siamese twins, congenital idiots. That's where it ends. With freaks and such."

"Is that your last word on the subject?"

"It's indecent is all I'm saying. Keep those sorts of things behind closed doors."

"Thanks for your thoughts, Cedar Falls. Now the rest of you, listen up. Don't ever say we didn't invite your point of view. We're in the opinion business. What you say to us on the air may offend us. It may titillate us. It may even make us mad. But we won't cut you off. The more controversial you are, the more we want you to call. All right? Do I make myself perfectly clear?

"Okay, you're on the air. Speak up."

"It's me and--"

"Wait, I know you. I recognize that voice. Am I right? Is it you again?"

"You were talking to me? Earlier you were? About losing my hair? You remember? I said I was bald?"

"I thought as much. How could I forget, Eagle Pass? Has something changed there?"

"No, just that--it's later now, if that's what you mean?"

"But not too late. You're still with us in Eagle Pass. That much is clear. What's your name?"

"Why do you ask?"

"It goes with the job. Give us your name so we'll know who we're talking to. That's the least you can do. Or better yet, put your grandmother on."

"She's not able to."

"We've heard that one before. What's your name then?"

"V.G. That's what she calls me. V.G. for Verda Grace. It's my name. Verda Grace is."

"Now we're getting somewhere. Go ahead, V.G. Speak your mind."

"That lady, the one before. She's wrong. I'm not a freak. She doesn't know me. How can she say that? I'm a person as much as her. I have feelings too, just like her."

"V.G. V.G. V.G. It takes all kinds, kid. You know that. Don't you know that by now?"

"I guess so, but--"

"Sure you do. Now, did you want to add something else to your earlier remarks?"

"Yes, but I don't know--"

"You're stuck on where to begin, V.G. Isn't that it?"

"You--"

"Try the beginning. How old are you?"

"Seventeen."

"Seventeen with a problem that needs attention. How am I doing so far? Could you say I'm on the right track? Getting hot, maybe?"

"Yes--"

"But you're feeling vulnerable right now and not ready to talk about it. I understand. It's hard sometimes when you're feeling alone and frail. But you're not alone, V.G. Everyone feels that way sooner or later. Relax a minute. Collect your thoughts. Take a deep breath while I do some business. All right? We'll get Bud Powell on the air yet. Just be patient while I pitch a few products that make all this possible. Here we go again, folks.

"I want to introduce you to a new process that dices your onions and slices those tomatoes without using a single watt of electricity. It's called the Slice-a-Fruit Rotary and works by simply pressing the top down with the palm of your hand. A turbine mechanism creates the rotation of blades that do all the rest. You can get it by sending us seven dollars, plus two dollars for postage and handling. Just order this miracle worker straight from the Night Hawk, Post Office Box Nine, San Antonio, Texas. And you will receive your Slice-a-Fruit Rotary in ten days. We can guarantee satisfaction.

"Now you're still listening to the Night Hawk on Radio Saltillo, XE *Anno Domini*, Coahuila, Mexico. Those call letters once more: XEAD, fifteen-twenty way out on the right of your radio dial. Everyone listening out there--in Ponca City, Topeka, Council Bluffs, and points north, city by city, farm by farm--you know the Hawk's theme song. When you hear 'Night Train' come up on the air, you know you're in for a treat. It's a promise you've come to expect and a promise we aim to keep.

"You know him, turned low so he doesn't disturb the rest of the house in the small hours of the morning, turned down so low you can barely hear him. You know him in one form or another. As an icy blast off Lake Michigan, as the shimmering, shivering Hawk of Lake Superior, whipping around the corner and going straight to the bone. You've also heard him as a tropical breeze wafting through the heavenly ether on the warm currents of XEAD or as a sirocco off the Sahara, warming the Mediterranean and the headlands of Italy. You may be working graveyard at the Acme Brick Works, stacking bricks in the small hours of the night as they come along the conveyor belt, loading baggage out at Love Field, waiting for the next flight to come in or take off. You may be a motel desk clerk out on IH-10, west of Las Cruces, a night auditor trying to get those figures to balance one last time. You may be a cotton hauler roaring through the night with a load of bales bound for the Port of Houston and a freighter at anchor due out the next day. You may even be on a train that woke my baby so far away.

"But wherever you are, whoever you are, you know the Hawk. You know him, one way or the other, a distant voice from the sky, the electronic correlative for what you're feeling at this very instant, down deep inside.

"Now I've got a caller on the line that's personally seen a diamondback rattler swimming in the Frio River. Tell me. Are we really ready to revisit that old conundrum?"

"It's no mystery, Hawk, those scaly diamonds, shining in the sunlight as it swam past me. I left the water in a hurry, you can bet."

"You were flummoxed, cowboy. Ever hear of a diamondback water snake? They're nonvenomous."

"No, that's a first."

"Well, look it up and call me back. Somebody please tell me what's this fascination with rattlesnakes in the late-night imagination? It's the leitmotif of the insomniac. This from J. Didion. Whether they can swim, I mean. All the way back, in 1951, the *Houston Post* credited Alex Binge with hooking a five-foot rattler while spooning for sand trouts below Matagorda. But if you want the final experience with such creatures, go to the San Antonio zoo. They got an albino rattler alive under glass, with a head big as a tennis ball, scales like plumage on a snow-white dove. Stare at its red eyes for long and you'll think you've been turned to stone by a gorgon's evil glare. You're on the air, Ozona, Texas. You a herpetol-ogist by any chance? There must be lots of rattlers in Ozona. You have any thoughts on the subject?"

"Are you there, Hawk?"

"Am I here? The Hawk's always here. Turn the radio off and focus on what you're holding in that hand. Who is this?"

"Donald Spooner."

"What's on your mind, Donald?"

"Me and Mrs. Spooner been running Harleys out west for twenty-five, thirty years. Closer to thirty, I'd say, and I believe it's finally destroying my kidneys and bladder, all that riding the highways."

"What makes you think so, Donald?"

"My stream's dried up to a trickle. As a boy, I took most honors putting it out there the farthest. But now I've lost the force I used to command."

"Let's bring Doc back in on this. Weak streams. Got an opinion, Doc?"

"Mr. Spooner, do you get up frequently in the night and feel you left the job unfinished when you go back to bed?"

"I do. What's that mean, Doctor? My bladder's going out on me or something else?"

"It isn't your bladder, Mr. Spooner. You have a tumor in your prostate, getting larger and larger, day by day. And the disease will kill you if you don't have something done about it. I don't mean to be blunt, but there it is, out in the light."

"Kill me?"

"If you don't get it tended to."

"An operation then?"

"Exactly. My professional advice is to get yourself down to Del Rio first thing in the morning and check into my clinic. Don't wait another day. And here's a word of advice, gratis.

"Don't think you can step into the first doorway you come to with a shingle and a caduceus. There are butchers in the world. They can get the tumor--I'm not saying they can't or won't--but they'll leave you incontinent. A man of your habits won't like wearing a nappy. But incontinence is an unnecessary embarrassment because my surgical procedure gets all of the tumor without touching the nerve. You'll have total control, be alive, and just as active as you used to be. So get over, with or without Mrs. Spooner. It's a matter of life and death.

"Now, I've got to leave you and get some sleep. Nobody wants a tired surgeon cutting on him. That's a wrap, Hawk. Keep up the good work. And just remember this. We're always at the Hill Country Clinic. You be there too. God bless and good night."

"Night, Doc. Get some rest and thanks for joining us and helping out. That's it for the doc, but before we go any farther, let me talk to the older people out there for just a minute. When we come back, we will pick up where we left off.

"Now if you're in your forties, fifties, or sixties and your mood's not what it ought to be. If the wife's nagging and you are just not as happy as you are used to, there's a little pill here called Florex'll make you feel like a young man again, and do the same for her too--make her feel like a girl again.

"It'll feel so good she'll be calling here nights, asking for one of these little nickel-head roach clips I have for you with my Night Hawk colophon stamped right on top. She'll catch those elusive little roaches by the wings and flip them right out the window when they're dead. That's how young she'll be feeling.

"One more time. If you've got something to say, give it to us. Air it out, right here, on the radio. The world's just waiting for your opinion. Give us a call. Okay, here we are, back again, and you're on the air. What's on your mind?"

"You cut me off before when there was--something I have to say."

"Let me guess. This wouldn't be V.G. again, would it?"

"Listen to me, please. Just listen to me this time."

"Fine, V.G. I'll give it to you. You're nothing if not persistent. What about your grandmother? Can she come to the phone yet?"

"That's what I have to talk about. My grandmother, who's not my real grandmother, though she raised me like one after my folks gave me up."

"What is it you want to say?"

"What I've been trying to say. Last night when she turned off the radio, like she does every night, after listening to you from midnight till you go off, she told me to fix breakfast."

"Your grandmother, who's not really your grandmother, told you to get breakfast. That what you're saying?"

"Yes--"

"Okay. So go ahead, V.G. You've already told us she did not give you the correct dosage, but what about the premium we sent along? Was she satisfied with the steak knives when they arrived? Before you answer, let's tell the folks out there what we're talking about here. Are you ready for this, night hawks? With every twelve-month supply of Detrichoma, you get a set of six heavy gauge stainless steel steak knives with oak handles and a counter block. If you'd like this beautiful set of knives, just order a year's supply of Detrichoma, writing to XEAD, San Antonio, Texas. That's San Antonio, not Saltillo. And with your Detrichoma, we'll send, at no extra charge, this beautiful set of steak knives and oakwood counter block to match."

"All right, V.G. How did your grandmother react to the cutlery?"

"She was surprised."

"At the quality?"

"By the sharpness. And me too."

"If she's a regular listener, she ought to know better. We handle only the best products available. The strongest Damascene steel for holding a sharp edge."

"Not only the sharpness. I was at the sink when she said I couldn't stay here anymore. She said I had to leave. I was no longer wanted because of the way I looked, a head with no hair and a face all puffy. She was done with me. I was to be on my own. That's how she put it. I didn't know what to say, and I was afraid."

"Afraid of being put out?"

"I was afraid of being alone."

"But then you'd be free to go anywhere, to do everything you wanted. Didn't you see that?"

"No, she got me confused, talking like that. All I thought of was her putting me out. Who would take me? And where could I go? People don't want girls with no hair. Men? It's okay for them. It's expected. But a girl like me--it'd scare the customers, even if I got a job. I could see that. She was sitting there, her wrapper on, in the chair beside the radio, where she'd been all night listening to you. Devoted to you, she was. Never missed a time. All night, every night. Bent forward, straining to hear if the signal faded, trying to tune out the static when it got too loud, a hot cup of tea by her, sweetened with honey.

"She told me to slice the ham with one of the knives you sent and fry it. But I was so paralyzed I couldn't do it, and she was cranky. So she started on me again. Kept at it, saying she was watching me. When she came over, all I could do was look at her. Then she raised her hand to me."

"Struck you? Is that what you're saying?"

"Not for the first time. But it surprised her how easy the knife went in. Me too, when it broke. How could you know? Before I mean. There was no warning, no reason to think it. Her mouth opened and she wanted to know why? It was her word, why? She just wanted to know why? Backing away, sitting down where she'd been all night, listening to you. I couldn't give her the answer she wanted any more than I can give it now. God knows I wondered too.

"Then I got more scared, looking at her in that dirty old wrapper of hers. Stunned. That's how she looked. Shocked, her mouth gaping. It caught us both off guard. She'd tell you the same. I believe it. I really do."

"What are you saying?"

"Just that I saw it was done and didn't know what to do. Until I thought of you. Call him, I thought. That's what she would do. So I've been waiting all day for you to come on. She was just sitting there with her look of surprise, and since you sent the steak knives I thought you would want to know. Without them it wouldn't have happened. I had to tell someone, don't you see? Are you listening? Is anyone listening to to me out there?"

"We're listening, V.G. We're all listening. So don't leave us. Tell where you live. Where in Eagle Pass. What's your address there? That's what you can do, V.G. Tell us where you are and how we can reach you. Can you do that?"

"Where am I? Here, on North Barranca. Seventeen North Barranca Street. It's the same address you sent the knives to. Where else would I be?"

"That's right. Now listen, V.G. Just stay there till someone shows. And don't hang up. Stay with me on the phone."

"It has to stop somewhere. I'm so tired. Waiting all this time for you to come on. You get tired--more so than you'd expect. It's been a long time, all day, all night, and I'm so tired. I'd better go now and lie down a while."

"No, wait a while, V.G. Don't go just yet. Are you still there? Are you still with us out there?"

"I can't do any more than I've done. Not for her. Not for myself. Not for anybody any more. I'm just too tired."

"Sure you can. You can stay on the line. You can do that. Are you there? Can you hear me?"

"I'm still here."

"Tell me how it happened. You say the knife went in and broke?"

"Yes."

"Can you be more specific?"

"When she hit me it broke the spell and I could move. So I did what she said and sliced through the ham. But the blade broke when it went in, and she wanted to know why I broke the knife. But I didn't do it on purpose. So I couldn't say."

"That's what happened?"

"Yes."

"Your grandmother's all right then?"

"She's upset."

"But otherwise okay?"

"Yes."

"Let me talk to her, V.G. I can explain that it wasn't your fault."

"That's not possible, Mr. Hawk."

"Why not? You said she was all right."

"She went to the court house to file a complaint."

"And hasn't returned? At this hour?"

"It happens sometimes. When she gets mad at me. She'll stay with her sister in town. Sometimes for days."

"And you think that's where she is. That's what you believe?"

"I'm sure she's listening right now. That's why I called. To say it wasn't my fault. Because I knew she'd be listening and I wanted you to help me out."

"Is that all you wanted? V.G.? Hello? It looks like we've lost her. She's off the line. But you heard what she said, night birds. You heard it right here. If you were thinking the worst you can relax. And if I seem-- out of sorts--well, you heard it too.

"You heard how it was said. Over the years I thought I'd heard it all. I've had interference crackling through the night, distractions of every kind. I've been disappointed and I've disappointed my share. I've been abusive and got it back as well. But that's my job. And I've been corrected for correcting others too much. But let me tell you if you don't already know it. You don't do this without some rancor out there. With a few surprises to boot. That's the nature of night. And who would know better than I? But I've never had anything like this before. I've never had such a night.

"If a certain grandmother is listening right now, if you're with a working radio and listening to us, and if I've got any pull with you, give me a call. Do you hear? Put in that call right away. I want to hear from you.

"Now, for the first time in all my years of broadcasting I'm going, under the circumstances, to dedicate a song to someone out there. If you're still listening--and you know who I mean--stay where you are. Don't touch a thing. I bet someone's grandmother is listening right now and will be home as soon as she can. So lie down, try to relax, young lady, try to be calm, and listen to the music. This is the one I've been promising all night. It's the one everybody's been waiting for. This is the one. Bud Powell's *Una Noche con Francis* and it's definitely for you, Verda Grace."

Hari-Kari

James White

Paul eyed the clock as he waited for the postman, hoping the stamped postcard he had left with his world literature professor would arrive. This spring semester he had an A in chemistry, A in French, A in physical anthropology, A in logic, but he had not heard about English. It should be his best A, but out of the blue, he had been in trouble in that class. A new Harvard Ph.D. taught it. Dr. McKiven had graded Paul low, even given him an F on the first essay. McKiven asked discussion questions Paul could not memorize or think out: How was the whale in *Moby Dick* like death in *Death in Venice*? Would Hester in *The Scarlet Letter* be an anti-heroine in today's society? Paul had held his breath whenever he handed in a paper. He had resorted to asking friends what the theme topics meant.

This summer he helped deliver furniture at his mother's and stepfather's main store in downtown Grand Prairie. They also owned two smaller ones that carried a lower grade of merchandise. Tonight, after work, he and Alice would drive ten miles to Dallas, eat moussaka and stuffed grape leaves at the Torch, then see a double feature at the high-ceilinged white and gold Palace theatre downtown. He was glad the semester had ended, and that McKiven was at least 180 miles away.

He sat on the puffy early American sofa, brass plaques hung on the dark green wall behind. The door was open wide and he could hear through the screen whenever the postman started up the sidewalk. He lay back against the flowered cushions. Tuesday and Thursday afternoons this summer he took a geology class from Professor Boone, the father of a high school friend, Johnny. The junior college would be a snap.

Paul got up, stood at the doorway, and spotted the postman on the Havarda's porch across the grassy boulevard. A minute more. The smell of gardenia floated through the screen, the bush in full bloom.

The postman crossed the lawn and started up the concrete walk.

Paul stepped back.

The postman couldn't see through the screen. The metal lid of the mail box made a noise as it was raised. The postman dropped in something, turned, and walked down the hot concrete. Paul waited for him to cross the yard, then he opened the screen door and took out all the different sized envelopes, a postcard falling onto the front porch. He leaned over to pick it up.

He went back inside and lay face down on the sofa.

A moment later he picked up the card from the cherry table, and read. *D. D.* No matter how much he disliked McKiven, Paul had recognized that he was stupid compared to him. All the students were. And to have the D exposed on a postcard for strangers to see. Those working in the post office. The postman. Paul tore up the card. For a moment he couldn't think.

He had just had to find someone smart enough to tell him he was dumb. This *D* was about judgment--everything had to be judged.

He threw the pieces of the card into the bottom of the kitchen garbage, then pushed in the round lock button of the front door, shut it and walked into the sunlight up to his convertible. He opened the car door and sat, putting the key into the ignition. He turned the switch and let out on the clutch, his fingers on the wheel. The tires rolled along. He swung a right at the corner, glancing at the rambling red brick house, then noted the white frame house ahead where a crazy person was rumored to have lived.

He had had A's like other students had C's in high school. He had had close to the highest grades his first semester in college. But now. He wished he didn't have to go to work. He couldn't sit in a movie with Alice tonight, either. How could he waste the time? He had no one but himself to deal with his feelings. He couldn't tell Alice or anyone. He suddenly thought that after work he would go to the library. He could be alone. He would read about intelligence, or philosophy or psychology. He was bright enough to learn what was what. He curved his hand over the knob on his steering wheel and began to steer with it.

He felt like he had when he had had to jump off the high diving board at Lake Kickapoo pool--afraid. Too soon he saw the store, his stepfather's last name lettered on the back wall. He turned down the bumpy side street to employee parking, got out and someone other than his usual self hurried inside.

As he walked in, he would have died if they had known. Ten minutes later, he rode beside Art in the delivery truck, Art looking down, alongside the fuming cars when the truck was stopped at a red light. "This one's got her skirt up," Art said, excited. "Look over here." Paul did. Before he went to lunch, Paul made sure to vacuum the flat grey carpet throughout the entire store. He emptied the ashtrays and dusted the new accessories, including a set of early American red ruby glasses he liked.

Later he secretly went to the phone and dialed Alice, saying that he could not go to the movie or have dinner with her family, he was sorry. Yes, he would call in the morning.

At five o'clock, he got into his car and drove the three blocks to the junior college library. Inside, only two or three other students studied, the rows of bare tables unoccupied. He asked the darkhaired girl at the desk where the philosophy section was located. She didn't know, but found out. There were few philosophy books on the shelves. The titles meant nothing so he chose at random. And he couldn't sit long in the wooden chair without padding. The room was no place to think. He would carry the books home. He checked out six, the maximum, then returned to his car. The campus was depressing because of how it looked. The two thousand students and the ill kept buildings created an environment as empty as a movie theatre with customers leaving after a bad film. His inevitable A in geology here would mean little. The lighted walk continued past the chemistry building to the lot behind.

Paul dropped the books into the trunk and drove home. He went into his room, shut the door, and lay the books on the rug beside his bed. So his nearly all A record was spoiled by a D. He lay down, his eyes closed to the ridiculous polka dot ruffled curtains his grandmother had sewn above the windows. He picked up a book and his eyes raced across pages, his fingers turning them again and again. He respected school and learning more than anything. People who wrote books had something to say, didn't they? And wasn't philosophy the apex of human learning? He needed to read something that exactly applied to him. Some insight. He set down that book and chose another. It concerned abstract, detailed points he didn't understand or care about. He tried one by Croce, then another. They rambled on and on, then became webs. Two hours later, he had piled them on the floor and his eyes stared at the ceiling of his room. Was this what philosophy was like? So interwoven and complex? Wasn't truth simple? He had looked up at the ceiling thousands of times, while lying on the bed. He was familiar with the eggshell white surface. He now hated looking at it, as if he had nothing better to do. He noticed a stain where the roof had leaked last Christmas. And the light fixture had a dark mess of bugs in the bottom.

A line he'd read in one of the books popped into his head and he leaned over, picked up a volume, and began to search for it. He skimmed several chapters where he thought it was. Finally he came across the sentence, "Constantly thinking about God, never putting him out of our minds, brings us closer to our true selves..." He eyes rested on the print a long while. The gears of his mind turned a notch. Our true selves. Yes, there were many selves inside him. He should remember he was not just a student. There was a reason why he studied to begin with. He reread the paragraph. "Brings us closer to...." Wasn't he looking for what was most important? Was thinking about God how to find it?

What if *he* tried to think about God constantly? What if he repeated God's name? Never let it out of his mind. God. God. God. God. Could he do that? Just repeat the word. What's really wrong with me? he wondered. He asked whoever God was as well as himself. Paul turned over on the loose, green spread. He faced the wall, his eyes open. God, he said to himself. Then God, God, God. Then God, God, God, God, God. Like feet pattering somewhere.

He entered a kind of privacy, saying it. It gave him someone besides himself to share his thoughts. He would have been embarrassed for anyone but God to hear.

He had had no thoughts of God for years. He could never be a holiness or a Baptist again. He rebelled against organized religion, vengeful gods, and conformity. He had never gone back to his grandmother's church where he had been a holy ten year old; after standing in a healing line that one summer in Haskell, he had put thoughts of God on hold.

Now here God was, when he needed him.

Paul repeated the word God in the back of his head while thinking this. Like background music. He could try to say it endlessly. God, God, God.

It was concentrated thinking. Once, vacationing uneasily with his parents in Washington State, no one in the car could agree on radio stations. Paul had sat in the back seat and decided to make up his own music. And he did. He listened for the long hours of driving each day during the rest of the trip, the music constant, wonderful. It often fitted the landscape as well as his thoughts. Then back home he had discovered that the music didn't go away. He had no off switch, and had had to learn how to hear nothing again.

He repeated God, God, God, God, God, God, God....until he felt relaxed. Could life be about finding God? Did he get a D so he could see beyond the importance of grades? The "God" he repeated became as if he said, "come back, please come back to me." He liked repeating it. God God God God God God God God God God God God.... The "God" ticked, a just wound watch.

Early the next morning he opened his eyes, yawned, then closed them. God. God, God, God. He remembered.

He got up, walked down the hallway, past his sister's room into the bathroom which was located next to the white tiled kitchen. He turned on the hot and cold faucets full blast. In the comfortable tub a moment later he said God, and relaxed in the steaming water, then, drying off, God, then five minutes later while eating cereal, God. God. God. God. Driving to work, he repeated God, God, God. Paul thought of molecules in the air. Every molecule of everything was God. How had he forgotten?

The people, houses, and cars, he passed on his way to work, did not exactly matter. His job didn't, either. He decided to call Alice and excuse himself again from coming over.

God God God God. God God God. God.

He entered the store, the bell at the top of the door, jingling. He passed the office, his mother speaking into the receiver, one silver earring on an index finger. Jimmie, the secretary, waved her red fingernails and he walked through the wide double doors leading into the back. The roll-up metal delivery door was raised and sunlight flowed in.

"We've got a sofa going to Arlington," Art said. He sipped black coffee from a clear glass cup. "And a bedroom suite."

"A triple dresser?"

"Yep."

Paul had dropped his end of one two weeks earlier as they were unloading.

He and Art loaded the furniture and got into the loud running white truck. Driving to Arlington, ten miles away, would help pass time.

God. God. Thinking it was easy. And yes, more important than thinking selfish things about himself. God God God God. Each word became part of an intricate design. Like grains of sand or flakes of snow or drops of water. God was environment.

135

"Did you fight last night?" he asked Art.

"I won." Art drew in his chest and flexed his tattooed bicep.

"Good."

After the delivery, they stopped at Mack's Cafe where Art flirted with Cynthia. Then they drove back to the store, got cool and started on the next delivery, a Sealy mattress and boxspring. This was delivered to one of the largest ranch style houses in town, which proved almost empty inside, only one sofa in the living room, pieces here and there throughout the rest of the house. The mattress and box springs looked lost in the master bedroom.

Then it was lunch and Paul walked down the street for chipped barbecue and an Orange Crush. He ordered a piece of chocolate pie with high meringue. God God God God.

He returned to the store and his mother called him as he passed the desk. "You didn't bring me any pie?"

"You didn't say you wanted any."

"I did, too," Jimmie said. "I wanted lemon."

"They had two big lemon pies," he said.

"How did you like Mrs. Heard's house?" his mother said. "Their furniture was repossessed by Owens and I told her she had to pay cash."

"That big house and they can't buy furniture?" He felt sorry for them. He couldn't have told Mrs. Heard. How bad she must have felt. Much worse than a poor person who couldn't afford something.

"I told you," she said. "A lot of those big houses you want are half empty. The people are just showing off."

"You look hot," Jimmie said. "Your face is red."

"It sure is," his mother said. "Cool off before you go back in the sun. And get us some pie in a minute. You can get yourself another piece."

Paul nodded and walked out through the back hall of the office, where supplies were stored. He went into the little stinking bathroom he had cleaned so much. He glanced at his bright face in the mirror. When she told him that he looked hot, he realized that his legs and arms and chest were covered with a perspiration that was dew like. It wasn't usual for him, even in this heat. God God God God God. He knew that he must fast. He must say no to all food. His eyes in the reflection were glinting.

White

The physical repeating of the word God was easy, but he began to notice certain side effects. He got very hot and he lost track of time. Repeating was compulsive, and the words he said did not calm him.

The next afternoon at the store Paul felt feverish. His stomach was empty. His head ached. The night before he had gone to Alice's to watch TV in the cramped living room with her, her brother Joe and her parents and then this morning, to geology class. Paul needed to memorize the Geologic Time Chart. Instead of his delivering furniture, his mother had asked him to work in the office. He knew how to post payments, figure the daily cash for the three stores and write collection letters.

He had repeated "God" without stopping for eighteen hours. It seemed only two or three minutes. How could other people not know to do it? He could not tell others to pray; they'd think he was nuts. They'd get insulted. Paul stood at the counter and took a payment from a woman in a low cut dress, then he walked down the hallway and into the bathroom. He closed and locked the door, alone with God. He glanced into the black speckled mirror.

There was no question that praying was affecting him. Was this person, underneath the layers of emotion, who he was? He felt his damp shirt, touched his hair at his forehead, then rubbed his wet fingertips together. He had no idea how high his temperature was. God, God, God. He turned the cold water handle at the sink, ran water onto his palms, splashed his closed eyes, then wiped his fingers on the back of his jean legs.

In the office, he sat on one of the brown padded chairs that rolled. He entered new deliveries into the inventory records. Jimmie glanced up, ready to talk more.

"Are you sick?" she asked.

He noticed his mother's face through the glass pane before she opened the door to the office. "Here's more tags," his mother said, and handed them to him.

"I just asked if he's got fever," Jimmie said.

"I'm not sick."

"I'll take your temperature tonight," his mother said. "Do you want to go home?"

He turned around and started punching in the numbers.

"Are you going to Alice's tonight?" his mother asked.

He nodded. He closed his eyes. Then he added in more figures.

He felt his mother's palm against his forehead. "You're burning up," she said.

"I'm not."

"Go on home," she said. They weren't busy. "Go on," she insisted.

Paul got up and left, the bell jingling. The hot brightness outside contrasted with the air conditioned florescent lighted store. He opened his car door and sat on the too hot to touch red seat. He would go home to pray. How wonderful to be alone. The word God was beautiful, like the sky. He started the engine and backed out, the yellow and black foam dice above the mirror bouncing.

At home, he entered his bedroom eagerly. He went straight to the twin maple bed that he always slept on by the wall. He lay face down. He put his hands to his head, his hair soaked, his arms and chest dripping. He covered his eyes with his fingers, his head trembling. God God God God. He could sleep now then make Alice's after dinner. Maybe he would tell her. In his dream that afternoon, he saw something green like a fly's eye peering into his and he turned away his gaze. He knew it was evil, and suspected it was inside himself.

Alice's parents didn't have money. They lived on Elder Street with the smallest houses in town with rinky dink porches, the lots cleared except for spindly trees the occupants had planted. Hers was yellow and ugly with brown trim. Her father kept the screen and door locked, and he either paced back and forth, smoking in the short hallway or he slumped in a green chair with wooden arms, one cheaper than any at Paul's parents' stores. Paul drove up to Alice's feeling more prosperous than they. He liked to buy her expensive presents--a cashmere sweater, a radio, a big stuffed animal. He got out, walked to the porch and Alice opened the door, her hair brushed, her pink shorts on her tan upper thighs. She wore a light blue blouse with corn flowers. Her hello meant she had been looking forward to his coming. He saw her brother Joe, ten, working on a project about Indians. Joe wore a headdress with feathers.

The dining room was a tongue from the living room and the table still had the pimento cheese and tuna fish sandwiches they served most every night, with a few sliced cantaloupe left on a plate. Her mother carried two glasses of sweet iced tea, clearing the table.

"Well, hello," her mother said.

A moment later Paul walked to the hall and into Alice's room. The tiny bedrooms had no insulation. He could hear anyone in her parents room next door even if they sat on the bed. All talking in the house could be heard by everyone. He lay on the polka dot spread. Alice sat down beside him. She began to stroke his straight brown hair. Paul gazed up, catching her eye, grinning. Then he began to stare into her eyes without blinking. He motioned for her not to look away. *Eyes*, he thought. What on earth? Eyes were not secretive. Her greenish irises had swarms of liquid movement, little things. His, too. He let his vision blur. Her eyes grew larger, distorted. He brought his head closer and put his hand on the nape of her neck.

"What are you doing?"

"Nothing." His nose almost touched hers. How could he tell her that just a few minutes ago as he entered the house he had sensed something evil? He was making sure it was not in her.

After a moment more, he sat up, then called, "Joe."

"You want Joe?" She was surprised. "Joe," she called.

He came in, blond hair askew. "Come here," Paul said.

Joe stood closer and Paul leaned over, looking directly into Joe's eyes. His nose almost touched Joe's. He let his vision blur and looked at the colors and forms inside Joe's sockets. Paul felt frightened. He looked for something he had never seen before, and he saw it, ahead, glaring back. Paul trembled. No no no God God God God God. A demon. The demon whose presence he had felt in the house was inside Joe. And he knew he had sensed others, not just in his mind. Others, around him, in other people.

"You look crazy," Joe said.

Paul pulled back and took a deep breath. He had to tell Alice about the demon. It would wreck Joe's life because he could not fight it. Joe was not protected. Paul knew.

He noticed Alice's hand against his forehead.

"You have fever," she said.

Joe went back into the living room.

Paul lay down, his head on her lap. "I'm trying to think about God every moment," Paul said. "If God is good, then I should. I have been for days."

"How?"

"I repeat the word. Every second, no matter what I do, I repeat 'God.'"

"How can you?"

139

"I keep it in my thoughts."

"Don't you have a geology test tomorrow?"

"I've sat in class. I know it."

"Isn't it a three hour test? How can you study if you're thinking of something else?"

"I can." He thought of the D. He almost felt glad for it.

Why had he seen a demon? Or did the demon exist? A worry settled inside his forehead. "I love you, Alice," he said. And he wanted to cry because his feelings about everything were so strong .

"I love you," she said, her eyes upset.

She couldn't understand. "I saw a demon in him," he said, his voice shaky. Alice looked very frightened.

The next morning as he drove to the test, the repetition of God was one with the turning of the tires. He noticed birds suddenly, high up, and flew with them. Far better to be in the sky than taking a test. He entered geology class, sat at a back desk and waited fifteen minutes for Professor Boone. When Paul held the exam pages, he sniffed the mimeo ink. Then he closed out the other students and wrote his answers. He looked up, minutes later, finished. He could not wait in the chair longer and with his sudden movement to get up, the boy beside him glanced over, curious. Paul walked to the front and handed Professor Boone his test. Boone raised up from his reading, his pipe smoking. "I'm finished," Paul said.

Professor Boone looked at his watch.

Paul saw that only twenty minutes had passed.

"Are you sure, Paul?"

"Yes." He knew it should take hours.

"I'll grade it, now." He took his red pencil and began. Paul's eyes turned away. He checked each right answer, Paul realized in a minute. Anything was possible. Another D.

"It's perfect," Boone said, genuinely surprised.

"Thanks." Paul left, his heart racing, and outside, he sat on the steps and closed his eyes. Relief. God's goodness was like light. He felt it. The goodness was all that made sense. He was sane if he could take the test so fast and make perfect. He was rational. He glanced up, another student about to enter the building. Get up, Paul told himself. Don't let anyone see you sitting here. As the student passed, Paul looked at him, then the features blurred, and one second, the boy shrank to a child of three, while a moment later, grew into a wrinkled old man.

Paul's fingers tightened around the keys in his pocket. Paul had seen Alice that way the night before, then had blinked and refocused.

He hurried toward his car. Did demons such as he had seen in Joe exist? Could he see these people at different periods of their lives all at once? God God God God. He was a little boat and his repeating God placed him on a stormy ocean. He looked up toward the sky, eyes squinting. What is this? he wondered. What is the sky, the ground, his hands, or his own ideas? What? What were things? What am I? he asked.

He knew no matter what else that he was acting on thoughts coming from inside himself.

That afternoon, sweat poured down his face as he stood in the air conditioned office. He added the petty cash.

"You need to see a doctor," Jimmie said. She touched her cold fingers to his forehead.

He didn't doubt her. "I'll go home when I finish," he said. He would be terrified to see Dr. Bobo, the family physician.

"You must have lost ten pounds," she said.

"I'm not as fat," he said.

At six that evening he and Alice drove the ten miles to Dallas. They decided to go to the movie at the Loma Alta theatre in Oak Cliff. First they went to a barbecue place, but Paul didn't eat. He drank several glasses of strong sweet iced tea. They walked along the small stores selling clothes and furniture and jewelry. Inside one was a photo booth. For one dollar they could sit in the booth and have their pictures taken and developed while they waited. Paul always had money and dropped four quarters into the slot. Then they sat back, making sure both their faces were framed in the photo. The flashes blinded him.

He liked the soft loose turquoise dress Alice wore with elastic holding up the top. The pictures took five minutes and unrolled at one time, the first appearing, the others scooting out behind. He took the three and held them up. Paul thought yes, he looked demented, his eyes slanting, very dark, almost glowing.

"You look romantic," Alice said. "Intense."

"Do I?" He watched her put them into her purse. Anyone who saw the photo could tell he was crazy.

White

Alice hooked her arm around his as they walked. He could see how happy she was. How could he tell her that he was afraid to close his eyes because of what he had begun to see--colored shapes, menacing reflections of teeth and eyes. Sometimes one of these things was Alice. They frightened him and he told himself, "you don't really see that." But he did. He saw demons outside his head too. Not often, but now, as they walked past a crowd he saw one with horns walking with a group.

He had never believed in demons. No one he knew did. He had trained himself all his life not to see them and now, here they were. You don't see a demon with the same eyes you see the world, he thought. Because to see a demon your world has to change already. Nor could he see one without God protecting him. If he did, the demon would go after him. He almost felt as if he had special information.

He began a prayer for himself and everyone he knew, then those he did not know, yet all the while, he talked to Alice whenever she spoke. She knew he was preoccupied. In the photograph, I look crazy, he thought. Why doesn't she say so?

The next morning in the bathroom beside the kitchen he turned the lock on the door and he sank to his knees. God help me, he thought. Goodness could not become what *he* thought it was because it had a nature of its own and it was his task to learn to see it. Beauty was not just the stars and the skies--it was heaven in his head, the peace, his need to let go of all the values around him and to listen to voices that could show him more about eternity. There was no need for him to be afraid if he loved enough. But he was afraid. Goodness was revealing badness.

God. God. Later he drove down West Second to Davis Drive to Abrams to the store. God. God. God. He had to get through work. He pulled into the parking lot at the store, got out and went in. The bell jingled. He passed the expensive furniture and continued to the office. He sat at one of the desks. He began to work on the inventory, but could not focus. He punched figures into the adding machine. Listen, he thought, I can't do this. He couldn't talk, either. And he became aware of a fear that he had not realized--of his mother, Jimmie, of Alice. The longer he prayed without stopping, the more aware he became of the gulf between this world outside and his. He closed his eyes, shapes swirling in the dark.

He did not talk all afternoon. At five oclock he left and drove home. He could go by Alice's later. He went inside, into his bedroom and got under the covers on his bed. He kept his clothes on.

He tried not to be afraid.

Suddenly he began to choke. He could hardly breathe through his mouth. He lay still, taking a breath, but it was shallow. A gasp came out with it. He did not want to be in that room or that house. He was being drawn into this awareness along with the absolute need to pray. He had to get away from the demons though and he did not know what they were or how to escape, if they were coming from his mind.

Nothing about his life pleased him or was suitable in order for him to praise God as he should. Why else did he have to hide his praying-- no one could see because no one could know. Wasn't it because there was no room for God in the ordinary things of his daily life? Did his mother really believe in God? Jimmie? Did Alice? If only they could understand!

God God God God God God. He drew the sheet up over his head. His forehead and arms and chest were soppy with sweat. His pulse was fast, making his head vibrate. He drew in, trying to breathe deeply.

Then he looked up--his bedroom door was opening. His mother had arrived home from work. It had to be six o'clock. She walked over to him; he could smell perfume.

She leaned down and kissed him. "You're burning up again."

"I can't breathe," he said.

"Oh, I'm sorry," she said. She walked across the room to the door and she went out.

She's sorry? And there was no air in his lungs, his throat or his mouth. His nose was closed up.

He heard the door again. Then, "Paul."

She had come back.

She leaned over his bed, a cool rag in her hand. She lay it across his forehead. "What's wrong with you?" She added, "I know something is."

It flooded from him. He had to tell. There was no one else to help. "If God is good, I should think about him all the time," he said. He was used to arguing with her, not respecting her opinion. His words now seemed ridiculous. How could he express what was happening? He sounded like an idiot.

"That's not right," she said. "You couldn't live if you did that. You'd go crazy."

He nodded. He knew this was sanity talking. He got his breath. Of course she was right. Finally, someone had told him the truth. Did he have a choice what to do? He had to accept her word, didn't he?

She was as large as life in front of him. He lived in this world, too. He should give up thinking about God. "Is that right?" he asked. Could I give up God, he wondered.

"Of course it is." She stepped back, then went to the door. "I'm going to fix supper. You'll feel better after you eat."

"Yes," he said.

The door closed. He felt his heart beating and tears began at his eyes. He did not know how to love God. How could he love and be afraid at the same time? He was so confused. Did thinking of God make him safe? No. He looked about his room. The word rolled in, over and over, into his head. God. God. Oh he loved Him! He slowed it. God. Then he made it stop dead. Something other than God began to speak. It was reality. Put your own thoughts back into your head, he thought. You have to live like everybody else. He didn't really want to. He wanted to know God more, to think of him literally. He looked at the furniture in the room, the window with the shade up, light flowing through. He remembered how simple things had been. Then, life had seemed undeniable.

He would eat, drive to Alice's and take her to the double feature. Just stop thinking about God. The D was no longer embarrassing. Who cared about a grade! He got out of bed and walked into the clean kitchen to see his mother. She faced the sink, and her dyed black hair was perfect. He knew exactly what she would say. He would not let his thoughts take their own course.

His life had been like an insect's.

His mind was not rock or air or flesh. It was decision, now in an avalanche.

Poems

The Junk in Grandpa's Barn

Walter McDonald

My brother swore that smudge in a photo
was Grandpa, sprawled by the train tracks.
We saw the puffs of smoke, the truck
crushed like a Coke can. Hogs he hauled

had to be slaughtered. After that wreck,
no one loved junk like Grandpa. Hobbled,
he puttered on trucks from junkyards.
Summers, we prowled bent grills and fenders.

Cracked windshields and motors littered the floor,
slick tires we rolled to each other.
Pigs rooted for pecans the bluejays dropped
flapping through the breezeway.

Pigs shoved blunt snouts into all dark corners
for mice. Often we heard a lunge and grunting
and smacking jaws, pigs faithful to junk
for their supper. Bumped by wet snouts

that sniffed us, we rubbed the crushed roof
of his truck, crawled in and cut our thumbs
on twisted tin, searching for blood. We squirmed
and cut our legs and wondered how Grandpa felt

cranking, pumping the pedal, stalled
on the tracks with squealing pigs to save,
a hundred tons of black steel bearing down,
the train's shrill whistle blasting.

L'Epervier: The Poet as Sparrow Hawk

Walter McDonald

He's grown cagey as a hawk,
no longer expecting meat dragged to him
by a sun stingy with shade. Coughing,
scoffing at himself, he takes whatever comes,
even weeks when nothing hops boldly

from burrows, when thermals hold him
over a world he's doomed by choice
and breeding to patrol. Sandstorms
or drought, he prowls hardscrabble fields,
throat dry as feathers in the wind.

He watches the plains for signs
worth diving for--jackrabbit's ears
above cactus, rattlers asleep
under mesquite twigs swaying
like arms, waving *here, down here*.

Jamaica

Angela Ball

The Mood Club is like the inside
of a hat oranged
with tropical dust, its rows
of rum bottles like the murk
of an old city. Jumpety table
made of old dark wood
for me to sit at and have
a bottle of Red Stripe.
There's something on the wall
behind me--spread thighs
framing my head, a mural of legs
scissored out so far the torso
attached to them seems broken
or sprung. Ashen patch
of dress, the rest
of the figure absent
or totally dark. A man
comes with dominoes, rubs them face down
on the table, and I get mine--
my favorite the one with a single
dot, slow black in all the whiteness.
He shows my thumbs how to command them
all at once to make a fence. Already he's way ahead
of me, eating my plays
alive, clacking down
his last domino--all the time moving
back and forth from the game
to his shaved ice concession
across the street--
he sells most of the color
electric blue. I lay down
more dominoes in a wide field
of split paths. "This one is rest,"
I say, "This one is sleep. Then love."
The man is silent, calm eyes.

He is the game. "Good shot" he says. There's ice
melting on the street: something glistening
into something dark.

L'Art de Toucher le Clavecin
Bach, after Couperin

Laurie O'Brien

He would have known that how you touch the keys
is a great deal like how you begin with a lover, a gradual
drawing back of the fingertips toward the flat
of the hand, giving the string time to vibrate
and then die away. He wanted the hands to oppose,
to converse, wanted a clear *obbligato* and a motion
slight and easy. Touch, he said, aimed chiefly
at a singing tone, *legato e cantabile*.

There were two wives. Maria Barbara, the organist's
daughter, he saw first in the Arnstadt church.
She was the one who died alone when he
was away, who was deep in winter ground before
he returned. So it is Anna, coming later, for whom
he wrote. *Poco allegretto*, orphan, he wanted
to dance, to put his fingertips up before her
and feel flesh, hear songs coming through her white hands.

At the organ manuals in the cold church he told
himself this was the way to tune--what?
his blood? his soul? *Jesu, Juva.* He
was alone with the sounds in the tall pipes pressing for air,
his mind a stream arguing for a voice.
Anna drew bar lines and careful clefs while Wilhelm
inked crooked notes. Light lay on their faces
in the same way it lingered over the great pipes
while he wrote. Grace, the little leading tones.
Mordent, how the notes turn with their quick little
shakes. Trill, a long run straight at the heart.

The Whale Watcher at Home

Laurie O'Brien

She has paid $2.75 for motherhood,
her share of the price of adopting Blizzard
and Olympia. Landlocked, she considers
them swimming in a far cold sea,
their glossy backs rolling over gray waves
before the plunge down into darkest water.
She would go there if she could. She would see
her babies big as schoolbuses, teeth like thumbs.
She would know them by their curved flukes
waving in blue air. She would recognize
their spouts, see how the water sluices
from their black skin when they blow.
She would learn their songs, then,
humming, swim beside them
into watery light like nothing
she had ever known.
She knows how she would nuzzle
a newborn, how her body might push
a calf with careful urgency up to where
silvered sunlight lies like oil upon
the surface of the world, up
for air and one quick look out
into where water ends.

Packaging

Hunt Hawkins

I remember old hardware stores,
dark places with bins of nails and bolts
and wrinkled proprietors who knew more
about your repair job than you did yourself.
This bright store covers half an acre
and has no one in it
except a sub-teenager at the cash register.
I need a single cup hook
but am obliged, it seems, to purchase four.
The sub-teenager won't break the package.
When I get home and store the extra three,
I discover three I had forgotten
sitting like little golden question marks.
And it's the same deal at the grocery store
where I have to buy six pears;
and at the clothing store, three undershirts.
Suppose I wanted a saxophone.
Would I have to get it in a four-pack?
Am I expected to purchase six chainsaws?
And how many coffins will they force me to get?
O America, turn back while there's still time.
You've already made me need things
I don't really want--my microwave oven,
deodorant, alarm clock, disability insurance.
Now don't make me buy things I don't even need.
Or is this some kind of package deal too?

Car Phones

What are they talking about, these men
with beige bricks pressed against their heads?
Business can't take that long.
Our cartoons have always painted women
as phone addicts, but these guys never quit.
Dodging my Rabbit to the shoulder,
I hope they're at least exchanging tips
on how to drive one-handed. Maybe they're
discussing their new-found ability to chat,
all calculation stripped away by motion.
Perhaps they're inquiring: Have you noticed
the green dots on the petals of snow flowers
in the first days of spring? They're recalling
the odor of bell peppers heated by the sun.
They're pondering what kinds of couples
love their spouses the most. And they're
remarking how night rolls back the sky
to reveal endless galaxies. Glancing out
their windows they wonder: Who are we?
Where are we going? They're grateful for
their phones which allow these questions
at last to be asked.

leaving
to a daughter

Betsy Colquitt

this time too you carry away things

--cuttings, succulents, rooted stems
that know to grow only where growing's hard.
will succumb in the kinless place
you're more and less settled in.

--and peppers too. you pack each kind,
hot, sweet, the temperate to toughened tongue.

--and always, something, old, forgot.
this time, a quilt top a peace-making old woman
i loved pieced of ties with strange patterns.

she'd have been your great-grandmother.
is, i guess, as genealogists count the dead.
i reckon more the knowing day by day.

--and always, the throwaways. brownies
should the plane fall and you need chocolate.
oranges for good vitamins.
a dr pepper--you like these.

your packing argues
distance is minor:
you can take the here with you.

my gathering says
distance is real, dangerous:
you can need help, do need reminders.

but we glean only a meager harvest
that wouldn't make a meal,

155

keep you one night in the Sierras.

at best, our rite reaps self-leavings,
a lore warming over how we were, are.
most, i guess, we try for something

we don't say: this letter home
that needs no posting.
this letter, if we wrote it,

would tell of love, trust, our wish
for safe journey to wherever it is
we each must go.

Body Bags

R. S. Gwynn

I

Let's hear it for Dwayne Coburn, who was small
And mean without a single saving grace
Except for stealing -- home from second base
Or out of teammates' lockers, it was all
The same to Dwayne. The Pep Club candy sale,
However, proved his downfall. He was held
Briefly on various charges, then expelled
And given a choice: enlist or go to jail.

He finished basic and came home from Bragg
For Christmas on his reassignment leave
With one prize in his pack he though unique,
Which went off prematurely New Year's Eve.
The student body got the folded flag
And flew it in his memory for a week.

II

Good pulling guards were scarce in high school ball.
The ones who had the weight were usually slow
As lumber trucks. A scaled-down wild man, though,
Like Dennis "Wampus" Peterson, could haul
His ass around right end for me to slip
Behind his blocks. Played college ball a year --
Red-shirted when they yanked his scholarship
Because he majored, so he claimed, in Beer.

I saw him one last time. He'd added weight
Around the neck, used words like "grunt" and "slope,"
And said he'd swap his Harley and his dope
And both balls for a 4-F knee like mine.
This happened in the spring of '68.
He hanged himself in 1969.

Jay Swinney did a great Roy Orbison
Impersonation once at Lyn-Rock Park,
Lip-synching to "It's Over" in his dark
Glasses beside the jukebox. He was one
Who'd want no better for an epitaph
Than he was good with girls and charmed them by
Opening his billfold to a photograph:
Big brother. The Marine. Who didn't die.

He comes to mind, years from that summer night,
In class for no good reason while I talk
About Thoreau's remark that one injustice
Makes prisoners of us all. The piece of chalk
Splinters and flakes in fragments as I write,
To settle in the tray, where all the dust is.

Poem for Barbara

John Gery

If not this year but several pass and you,
a blue and uneventful ocean view
lacking even the gesture of a sail
my mind might gather in in small detail,
still feel invisible, despite that I
intently gaze at you, as at the sky,
a breathless sky above the water, clear
and gentle in its rise, yet flush with fear,
don't think me self-absorbed, intransigent,
or cool. Were it enough to be content
with living with one whom I could recognize
as sometimes beautiful, or one whose eyes
assuaged my long-tormented soul, I'd say
as much -- I'm tempted even now to stray
from my not saying such, to wax sublime,
to batten down your beauty with a rhyme
or two and let that be my celebration
not of you nor the sea, this brief vacation
from the truth, but of me for thinking so.
I can't dismiss what I'm not thinking, though:
You're not what I expected, so the shore
I stand on, as fragile as the weather, more
or less replaceable, depending what
the sea delivers, sinks into the rut
of its own undoing, down, down, down.
Whatever words set sail upturn and drown
under the waves of your otherness, while here
in the dormant air, I stare at what is near,
missing each arc, the muffled cry of gulls,
the shifting tides in you, the rage, the lulls.

From the Gulf

Peter Cooley

High summer the clouds here are motionless,
they have nothing to do with us,
the lives we chose. Over the water
they roll back mornings tapering
at their ends, flecked like eggs
a giant sea bird warmed & fled.

And the palms, how quietly they bend
their shafts through white heat, trembling
the upper branches, quivers
in the noon's calm. How strange
at the beach each of us appears
naked to ourselves & yet a body

Greek deities took on in stone.
While from the surface of the ocean,
at evening, shaking off the foam,
the fixed stars' stare has risen
with their reflections, found their names,
light, light & nothing we can be.

Locales

Peter Cooley

After the last gulls, the scavengers
for Florida shells, the couples leaning
years on each other, after teenagers
leaving the beach the angles of their thighs,
the shark boat shrilling its all clear finally,
the clouds turned, sterns to leeward
across the gulf, a trawl of white fire
stretching to Texas.
                              And there they stood,
two boys straddled by two girls
sexless before adolescence, fully clothed
in black, disguised all afternoon
as shadows on the whitecaps, shallows
of their robes like priests', the full skirts,
long sleeves, swollen, dark with water.
And then they turned, themselves again,
children of the Mennonites, washing me up
on sand still warm before the clouds
lifted, put out to Mexico.

Among Cherry Blossoms
for my sister Ann

Leo Luke Marcello

Under cherry blossoms I picnic on the grass,
watching the sun sink into the Tidal Basin,
while I sip wine and eat spinach pie,
the horizon nibbling away
the sweetest moments.

Grandpa never saw cherry blossoms.
Whenever he called us his little flower garden,
I imagined roses of every color, bright daisies,
irises, here and there a tall gladiola,
and in the thick lush green some wildness,
all surrounded by a gray or white fence.
The fences have fallen, Ann,
our full lives wild with flowers.

Did he foresee more of this world than Washington,
that first glimpse beyond his beautiful, violent island
north in the cavalry warring past industrialized Milan?
Later, worn, returning home, down through the sole
of his torn country, he chose to sell everything,
and abandoning grief he sailed from Palermo
with parents and sister and her orphaned children.
They forgave their island its violence,
but they never looked back.

In the New World he wandered New York for days
searching in the wrong language for the houses
of brothers and friends who had gone before.
Eventually in a new south they built homes
and planted gardens and fig trees, now old.
Four of those six are buried there.
The only one left still
faithfully tends her garden

and sends me gifts of dried oregano,
mint, and *basilico*, perfumed bags
as exotic as frankincense, magic
for the sauces of our family's past.
I eat pasta and I think of her.
What is it like to be the last?

Sister, we can't think of one another dead,
but if you are the one who lasts longer,
I hope you'll revisit this memorial
and remember in the shimmering world
that we have laughed together.

There were no blossoms
that hot summer day years ago
when we climbed the white steps,
unimpressed by old bronze Jefferson
but happy to play in his shade,
laughing at our powerful echoes.

Under the dome children still explore
their shadows with the latest cameras,
but now the blossoms have arrived,
small dancing shadows across marble.
I don't remember so much water.
If the world is supposed to shrink,
for some reason, this one hasn't.

Things happen.
We grow old in different cities,
our lives filling to the brim.
We didn't foresee the hard miles,
the wrinkled years and scarred hearts,
maps creased and refolded into fringe,

or the joy of the longed-for and found,
like a brother's home in a new city or
the enjoyable conclusions that keep sending us
back to their beginnings for more. Or elsewhere,
old immigration papers in strange, flowery script,

a heavy silver chain without its watch, and
in the yellowed Italian prayerbook, a faded shamrock,
rediscovered, rekindles light among holy words.

This Park

Jeffrey Goodman

The long-eared rabbit ventures into grass,
Intrudes upon this pallid, lonely park;
Pure primps a white front paw, quiet and crass,
Where nothing's his and nothing is not dark.

Edges the rising pit and pulse of steam:
Pert, pulsing, oblong mouths jig flowers of ice.
The settlement of fog occludes the stream,
And the live oaks bend, the stepping stone dries.

In pale, burnt nests that thin like rabbit bone,
In the leaves where squirrels stray, frail and dense,
The migratory lift scum, lye, and stone,
Shaking white air, skimming dark thorns leaves fence.

In frills of solvent sky, above pale ground,
Their V-shaped wedge now like a dot in space,
Cold honeybees there swarm and there surround
The innocent with numb and savage grace.

And in November I seek solace where
A line of traffic ants divides the plain
Of dust with steady patience and cold care
While sickened nights extort the greedy rain.

Staying Lost

Jim Clark

Sometimes I walk
until I am gone from everything I know

I walk and walk
but something keeps tugging at me
some memory I think

I look back
and see I am unraveling
already an arm is gone
and half the shoulder

I walk faster and faster
thinking maybe I can make it
before I am all gone

I try to trace the web
back through its tangles
but only lose more of me
as I turn in the circles of the lost

Finally my feet vanish
and I stop
strung like a net from rock and tree

So this is how it is
to be lost everywhere
like a spool of nerves
spun through the body of the world

From a thousand trees and bushes
I feel the delicate tremor
of birds weaving their nests

Winter Flight

Jerry Bradley

In November when the weather is bad
geese begin their squabble on the lake.
Their wings spiral through the mizzle
like the smoky eddies of chimneys,
memories as hazy as laid eggs,
and orbit the turbulent, entropic waters
billowing south through the roil
at right angles in the sky
heading like transients for the border.

When tomorrow clears the winds
these evicted feathers will sit elsewhere then,
cries trailing through the failed season
like felons or threshed grain,
and the air will be full of misgivings
where their call -- *relent*! *relent*! --
breaks like feathery stemware in the storm.

Margarita

Jerry Bradley

Margaritas are my drink for luck,
their briny brims the taste
of sweat after love and stems
like the legs of starlets
frozen in the moment
before they open in all my dreams.

In Mexico when we drank our healths
I kept us all well, the ones
who'd tossed their hearts like dice
and stood eyeball with the snake
or been ridden like boxcars to the grave.
We cursed our scars but kept pistols
in the car to be safe.

Absurd and possessed, we drank through
heedless youth and lived. Now
we drink for luck -- good,
bad, and indifferent --
and to waken to find you here
is to taste again the curious heart
          of cactus on my tongue.

Long Distance Heart

Allan Peterson

What we cannot seem to do is believe in each other
over long distances. A few days and we're uneasy.
A few months and Hank sends Julie a note from the lawyer.
When he clears the dead vines out of the arbor he thinks
their paths are like the distant suspicions of the heart and feels
what he cannot hear for his own good any longer without holding
   hands:
the throbbing in the thumb of the princeps pollicis
and between their fingers grasping vines of palmar interossei.
He's become equally certain no one's in the universe and if there were
he couldn't trust them. Even blood at the far ends of the body must
   return
to believe in oxygen then question its intentions.
The latin heart cardium opens its extra rooms and the atria
with the padded hammers they hear at night through their bedsprings.
If there were anyone out there they would have their own peevish god
and in the living room he tells that story how she felt so bitter
she needed to split off like rivers of blood around the ears as the carotid
forks like Niagara till she couldn't hear him or thunder above them
or anyone's story of creation and neglect. If we had to listen we'd all go
   deaf.

The Pratt-Mont Drive-In

Jeanie Thompson

i.
You must enter the tattered drive
past a fountain of lights,
stilled now at midday.
Take in your hand the rusted chain
and heft of padlock, then step over.

You were always here at twilight,
twirling with your brother
on the tilted, spinning playground disk.
Skinny arms holding on, your head hung back
and you saw the world upside down,
dragged a foot where foul water pools now.
Back in the Ford, you peered over the seat,
then dozed, dreaming a succession
of tail lights and the screen returned to silence.

ii.
You seek the detail
in corners, the shafts of light,
the exact angle of the exit signs
that repeat after each row.
And the big screen, its placards separating
against a backdrop of humid, milky sky,
blank, offers nothing.

Ask yourself the question,
add the details again and again.
See yourself driving in at 8 o'clock,
autumn, the car warm, the boy
ready for anything. Smell the first
cigarette, the beery taste of his lips,
the soft focus of men and women larger than life.
And you, holding your breath, wondering,
how long did that kiss last?

Bone Bearers

(Upon Hearing Edwin Honig Read)

Sue Walker

Caught in niggling time, Edwin Honig,
you defy minutes, hours,
the break of light that fades.
Your voice summons the dead
sleeping their after-bone.
Why bother them?

Spare them translations;
they have no need of native tongue
to set the order right.
But on a March-mud afternoon
when rain outside washes poetry
from easy reach and grasp,
you clasp your tiny brother's hand
and yank him back
where he'd never want to be,
tread him through time
until--as an old man fearing blindness,
stumping a walker as he goes--
he'd welcome a kettle-whine.

I know. I'd grab my father
but two weeks dead
straight from his grave-
for my sake. And were he home,
I'd listen to his tales of "Old Joe"
whose back never tired to bearing
a boy to meet an engine coughing steam.
I'd take my father's hand
in mine, squeeze it tight
and speak of how I love.

We poet
our kennings of grief
carry baskets of bone
too long
too far.

Two Poems: Minimalism and
Quitting Smoking After 30 Years

Walt Darring

Minimalism

Wary by nature, with heels up-
lifted in midstep by the ears
to catch an ego-
      tistical nuance as it appears
      on my lips and hush it-- *hup*!
           we told me so;

my baby tries a late night trans-
it on round bones slowly, slowly, so
no voice can cry:
      what's that? who's there? you?
      It is all things, pure chance,
           nobody, why.

Quitting Smoking After 30 Years

No one savoring the illusion
Of immortality can understand
Why one one's own will will command
To countermand one's own desire,
Or why one cools with indecision
Before one reaches one's conclusion--
Which has been symbolized by fire.

The Milkmaid

Diane Garden

--after Vermeer

For just a moment she has shed
all her troubles: the cow going dry,
her daughter's wheezing. She has let
it all fall away till nothing matters,
but the cold and stubbly pitcher against
her hands, her basket filled with bread
and light. She knows her body fills
the narrow corner--that she can touch
the wall that's bare and cream-colored,
the windowpane speckled brown like a bird,
that nothing matters, but the milk
falling in a braid to the russet bowl.

The Hour of Fear

Rainer Schulte

Ships that have travelled
across the ocean look for anchors
in harbors
where dead fish
with hollow eyes
drink the water

Whoever steps forward
looks like a poster
that has not found
its place on the wall.

Behind the walls
dark impotence
bites its own head.

And we who have to go on
living
collect dead fish
on the shores of tomorrow.

Scars

Sheryl St. Germain

Today the streets run like gray scars
across the cold face of this city.

I love the scar on my stomach that runs fat
and long where they cut my son out;

I touch it at night sometimes, I like to feel
how the skin is different there, protruded and smooth

something happened here
the body heals itself, we change,

grow older, are not gods,
and a poem is a scar, not the wound

itself but the knowledge
of the wound, the flag

of the wound, a wiser tissue
laid out like a street, *this way, this way.*

Coastal

Sheryl St. Germain

You have been too long land locked,
too long in the libraries of scrub
and cactus, droughtened, predictable
lands without the smell of your birth.

Maybe it is the wind
that suddenly awakens you--
like a slap it lifts
the ocean to you, it is
the smell of your mother,
of some infinite longing, of sex,
of shells and bones sun-white
in their death and crab smell.
Salt, fish and the sands
with their infinitesimally
small bits of broken shell
and gut and bodies and hearts.
Sea smell of something dead.

Familiar, like family,
this haphazard meeting of
land, sea,
The sea like milk,
the coast your body.

Contributors

Stories

Ewing Campbell teaches at Texas A&M University and has published widely.

Tommy Franklin recently won first place in the *Nebraska Review* Story Contest and teaches at Selma University.

L. Jean Gardner, a psychologist, recently published her first book.

Tim Gautreaux has a story included in *Best American Short Stories 1992*. He teaches at Southeastern Louisiana University.

Trellie Jeffers teaches at Talladega College and is working on a novel.

Joanna Leake, director of the Creative Writing Workshop at the University of New Orleans, has published the novel *A Few Days At Weasel Creek* and has sold screenplays.

David Madden directs the Creative Writing Program at LSU. He has published a number of novels, and this excerpt is taken from his Civil War book *Sharpshooter*.

Scyla Murray, a young writer in Mobile, is an All-American in track.

Jim Sanderson teaches at Lamar University and won the 1992 Kenneth Patchen Award.

Les Standiford's latest novel *Done Deal* was recently published by Harper Collins. He directs the Creative Writing Program at Florida International University.

Jeff Todd, from Biloxi, Mississippi, coordinates The Fairhope Conference and is working on a new novel.

Erika Corey Turner, a graduate from UC-Berkeley, is from Florida.

Novelist James White directs the Creative Writing Program at the University of South Alabama.

Allen Wier, former Director of Creative Writing at the University of Alabama, has published widely.

Miles Wilson's story collection *Line of Fall* won the John Simmons Short Fiction Award at Iowa. He directs the program at Southwest Texas State University.

Poems

Angela Ball's poetry collections include *Kneeling Between Parked Cars* (1990) and *Possession* (forthcoming 1994). She teaches at the University of Southern Mississippi.

Jerry Bradley, a Texan, is the new Dean of Humanities at Indiana University Southeast.

James Clark of the University of Georgia has published widely.

Betsy Colquitt's books include *Honor Card and Other Poems*. She directs Creative Writing at Texas Christian University.

Peter Cooley teaches at Tulane University. His books includes *The Room Where Summer Ends* (Carnegie Mellon).

Diane Garden's poem "The Milkmaid" won 2nd Place in the Alabama State Poetry Society Poet's Laureate Contest in 1992.

Walt Darring recently published a new book of poems entitled *My Life's Work*.

John Gery, author of two poetry collections, is Associate Professor at the University of New Orleans.

Jeffrey Goodman has published in the *Southern Review* and *Chicago Review* and teaches at Spring Hill College.

Sam Gwynn has published widely and directs Creative Writing at Lamar University.

Hunt Hawkins, Associate Professor at Florida State, won the 1992 Agnes Lynch Starrett Prize for his book *The Domestic Life*.

Poet Leo Luke Marcello won Teacher of the Year last year at McNeese State University.

Walter McDonald is Paul Whitfield Horn Professor of English and Poet in Residence at Texas Tech University. His recent books include *After the Noise of Saigon* (UMass) and *Night Landings* (Harper Collins).

Laurie O'Brien teaches Creative Writing at the University of West Florida. Her book *Rogues Codes* has been accepted for publication.

Allan Peterson, Chairman of Art at Pensacola Junior College, has had a National Endowment Grant for Poetry.

Rainer Schulte, Professor at the University of Texas-Dallas, has published a number of books.

Sheryl St. Germain teaches at the University of Southwestern Louisiana. Her books include *Going Home* and *The Mask of Medusa*.

Jeanie Thompson is a founder of the Alabama Writer's Forum. Her books include *How to Enter the River*.

Sue Walker, publisher of *Negative Capability*, teaches English at the University of South Alabama.